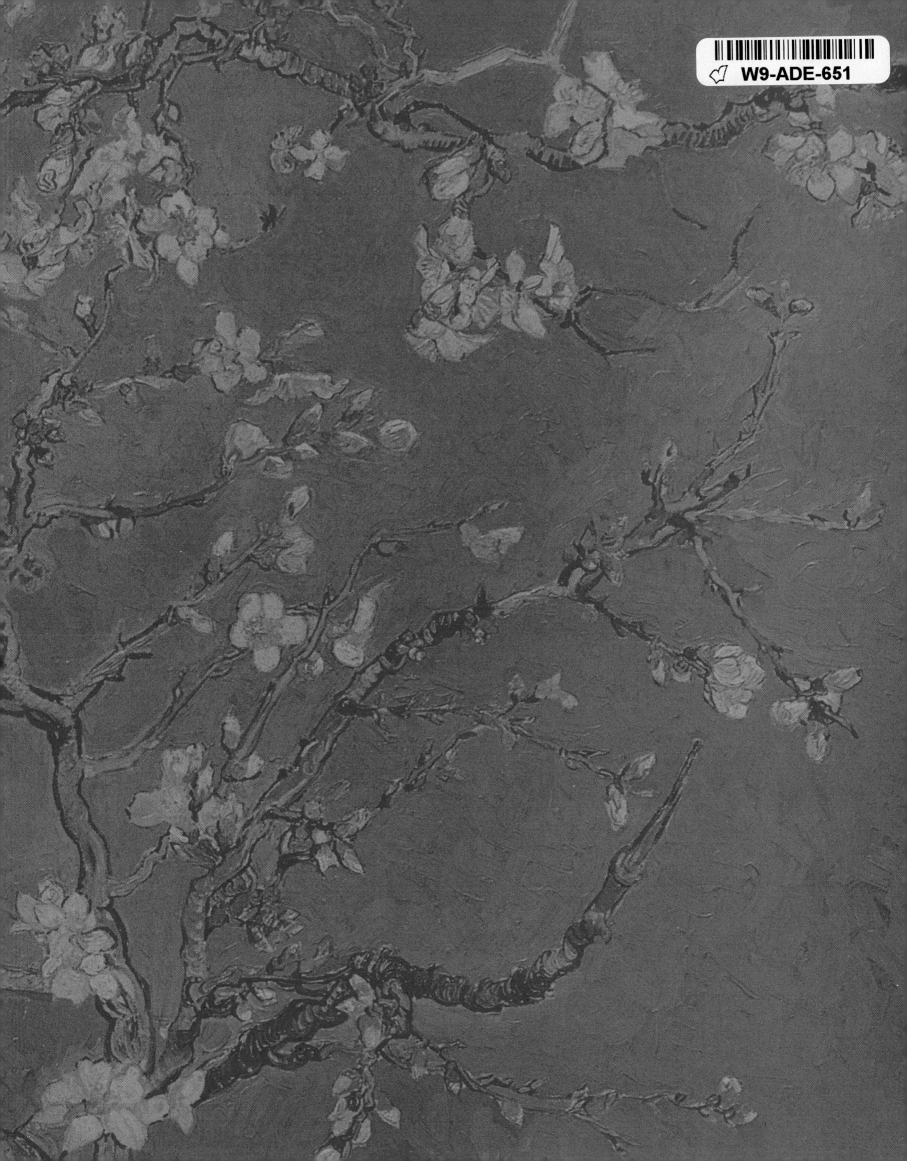

VINCENT VAN GOGH

Jörn Hetebrügge

VINCENT VAN GOGH

1853–1890

Bath · New York · Singapore · Hong Kong · Cologne · Delhi · Melbourne

CONTENTS

I. MOVING TOWARD ART (1853–1880)

MOVING TOWARD ART

There are only three photographs in existence of Vincent van Gogh, one of the most famous painters of all time. The earliest one shows him with short, thick locks and rather soft features, a boy of thirteen who looks rather shyly into the camera. In the second photograph, which dates to the beginning of his apprenticeship as an art dealer, Vincent is nineteen, now grown up to be a young man, with a forceful demeanor and a prominent brow. The only picture that survives from van Gogh's period of artistic creativity reveals little of the artist's physiognomy: Vincent is seated at a little table on the bank of the Seine River with his friend, painter Emile Bernard, with his back to the observer (illus. foldout timeline).

Nonetheless, we have a fairly accurate picture of what van Gogh looked like. Artist friends such as Henri de Toulouse-Lautrec and Paul Gauguin made portraits of him (illus. p. 10, p. 145). Most importantly, however, he painted himself time and again, and to a large extent, it is these self-portraits that have shaped the public conception of van Gogh's physical appearance. The images are noteworthy because they are certainly not realistic representations in terms of trompe l'oeil technique, but rather stylistic finger exercises, aesthetic statements, and self-analysis in equal measure. However, the fact that they replace a paucity of photographic evidence appears virtually emblematic for the awareness of van Gogh as a person and for the reception of his work. The artist's life and work are so intertwined that were it not for his paintings, Vincent van Gogh might hardly emerge as a figure.

Paradoxically, the overlapping themes of his life and work are both the key to the "van Gogh phenomenon" and the prerequisite for the origin of the "Vincent myth." But it was his sad tale of apparent insanity and of suicide that led him to become an idol in Parisian intellectual and artistic circles, a seeker of truth who gave up his life for art. This mystification also made van Gogh a candidate for more widespread fame, and thus the culture industry attended to it early on, and wrote the legend of the lonely genius painter on the brink

Vincent van Gogh at the age of nineteen

Pages 6–7
Planting Potatoes (detail), 1884, oil on canvas,
27½ x 67 in (70 x 170 cm), Wuppertal, Von der Heydt Museum

Self-portrait with Straw Hat and Artist's Smock, 1887,
oil on cardboard, 16 x 13 in (41 x 33 cm),
Amsterdam, Van Gogh Museum

"A figure more wide than long, shoulders slightly and habitually stooped, head hanging down, reddish blond hair cut short under a straw hat that casts a shadow on a strange face; not the face of a young man. The brow already wrinkled, the eyebrows knit in deep meditation above the wide forehead, small deep-set eyes, sometimes blue, sometimes green. Even with such an unattractive, awkward presence, there is nevertheless something remarkable in his distinctive expression of inner depth."

Elisabeth Huberta about her brother Vincent, 1910

Henri de Toulouse-Lautrec *Portrait of Vincent van Gogh,* 1887,
pastel on cardboard, 22½ x 18⅓ in (57 x 46.5 cm), Amsterdam, Van Gogh Museum

Vincent's brother, Theo van Gogh   Vincent's father, Theodorus van Gogh   Vincent's mother, Anna Cornelia van Gogh

of insanity. This cliché has lost very little of its attraction to this very day, despite the different picture that has emerged in recent decades as a result of scholarly research into van Gogh's life.

Vincent's exceptionally close relationship with his brother Theo has also fallen prey to romanticization. This unusual sibling relationship has left a record behind that has long provided comprehensive, vast, and undisguised insight into van Gogh's life and work, whatever problems there may have been with the history of its publication. The brothers kept up a detailed, lengthy, and nearly uninterrupted correspondence for eighteen years during which they exchanged letters about private matters and, above all, about art. Vincent's letters constitute the primary source material for this book and should be regarded as works of literary merit that, over the course of hundreds of pages, provide detailed information about the circumstances surrounding his artistic develop-ment and the creation of his works, thus refuting the image of the raging artist. They vividly demonstrate that van Gogh's career path—whatever fascinating consequences may have dogged it, and however contradictory it may have been— was the result of intensive, stringently controlled reflection.

It was van Gogh's desire to break new ground in art, yet without claiming for himself that he had attained that goal. No matter the extent to which van Gogh's visionary work is infused by an immediate and explosive power, it at the same time is the result of his irrepressible diligence and astonishing discipline, having its roots firmly in the "Protestant" work ethic of the son of a clergyman from Brabant, Holland.

CHILDHOOD IN BRABANT

Anna Cornelia van Gogh, née Carbentus, brought a healthy son into the world on March 30, 1853, in the parsonage of Groot Zundert in North Brabant, who would shortly thereafter be baptized Vincent Willem. This was a happy ending to a tragedy that had taken place exactly one year beforehand, when the wife of Protestant pastor Theodorus van Gogh had given birth to a stillborn baby boy. This sad occurrence would have received little enduring notice if the parents had not entombed the little body in the graveyard with a memorial plaque that bears the name of their first child: the dead child was also named Vincent.

This bizarre connection to a stillborn brother of the same name has always fired the imagination of biographers and interpreters. It has both promoted the mystification of this artistic genius and helped to explain van Gogh's personality in terms of traumatic childhood experiences. The belief that Vincent's existence had been ill-fated from the beginning is an integral part of the "van Gogh myth." Ultimately, the fact that little is reliably known about his early years changes nothing—quite the contrary.

As a matter of fact, there is evidence that Vincent experienced a boyhood that would have been entirely normal for the son of a middle-class country pastor in nineteenth-century, Calvinist Holland. Conservatism, industriousness, and modesty were the moral cornerstones of this social milieu, which not only led many people of sensitive temperament to experience its condemnation of sensuality as formative, but also caused them to feel repressed. The rather sparse reports about the young Vincent, which emerged at a much later point in time, describe him as something of an outsider, mainly kindhearted, polite, and introverted. At the same time, they also reveal that he could be willful and short-tempered within the family. This, however, does little to prove his eccentricity.

Anyone who heads for Zundert to look for traces of Vincent finds that few authentic places remain from the period of van Gogh's childhood. Only the Protestant church with the cemetery and aforementioned grave seem to have survived the passage of time. The family home across from the town hall on Marktplatz, for example, is long gone. A photograph shows the old parsonage of the Reformed congregation to have been a small white building in typical rural style with a simple decorative gable, which appears to have offered little space for the many members of the pastor's family, at least by today's standards. Vincent certainly did not remain an only child. His siblings Anna Cornelia (1855–1930), Theodorus ("Theo," 1857–1891), Elisabeth Huberta ("Lies," 1859–1936), Wilhelmina Jacoba ("Wil," 1862–1941), and Cornelis Vincent ("Cor," 1867–1900) came after him. Later in his life, though, Vincent seems to have remained close only to his brother, Theo, and to Wil.

Although they belonged to the elite of their village and were well thought of among the Catholic majority, the family lived in rather modest circumstances. The father's salary did not allow for any major advancement, and the crowded rooms in the parsonage must have ensured that his profession permeated daily life within the family and defined life in the home. But Theodorus was not a dogmatic pastor. He was a member of the Groningen Party, which represented a more liberal form of Protestantism than the prevailing orthodox

During my illness, I saw every room in the house in Zundert in my mind's eye, every path, every plant in the garden. . . It's because I have earlier memories of those first days than the rest of you. There is no one left who remembers . . . but mother and I. . . . it is better if I don't dredge all of that up again. [573]

Vincent van Gogh to Theo, January 23, 1889

Calvinists. For the "Groningers," the role of Christ was at the center of their faith. They saw him as an exemplary man—not as God. Theodorus consequently saw his role as a clergyman in the province primarily in terms of active care, mission, and education of the rural population and was involved in the social concerns of the peasantry, which must have had a deep impact on Vincent. Theodorus was both a beloved father and a role model to the adolescent. The decisive impetus of his early years was to emulate the patriarch of the family and to win his approval. Although the pastor's eldest son later recognized the difference between ideals and reality full well, and therefore more or less openly rebelled against him, the ethical foundation that Theodorus imparted to his son continued to be of fundamental importance to Vincent, the artist, as did a spiritual world view. Van Gogh's deeply religious sense is central to understanding both the man and his work.

Planting Potatoes, 1884, oil on canvas,
27½ x 67 in (70 x 170 cm), Wuppertal, Von der Heydt Museum

Anton Mauve *The Harvest*, watercolor on paper,
17¼ x 27¼ in (45.3 x 69 cm), The Hague, Haags Gemeentemuseum

Theodorus van Gogh came from the middle class, as did his wife, the daughter of a bookbinder from The Hague. He followed in his father's footsteps by becoming a pastor. Three of his brothers instead pursued careers as art dealers, another tradition in his family, which was considered an extremely respectable profession in the Netherlands, where private art collecting among wealthy merchants had been a common practice since early modern times. Theodorus' brother Vincent (who was called "Cent" within the family) excelled as a partner in Goupil & Cie, one of the most important, nineteenth-century Parisian art dealers, and brought them considerable renown and prosperity. Cent's nephew, also named Vincent, would later take his first steps into the art world as an apprentice at the company's branch in The Hague.

The family environment in which Vincent grew up was undoubtedly open-minded with regard to artistic matters, although tastes surely must have run toward the conventional, and art must have been viewed from a distinctly economic perspective. At the parsonage, art was also accorded an educational role in the Christian sense, and its value must presumably have been defined to a significant extent by its ethical content. Even so, paintings were clearly part of the home decor. Even the mother of the house sometimes picked up a pen and brush to draw or paint. Whether Vincent showed any signs of budding artistic talent as a child is unclear, however. Several sheets that had once been regarded as possible childhood drawings are no longer attributed to him today.

Theodorus taught his eldest son to value nature. His receptivity to the austere beauty of the landscape was awakened on walks through the moorlands of Brabant, and Vincent later recalled it even more sentimentally because the original images were on the verge of disappearing. More and more farmland was lost to urbanization, and farms were more intensively cultivated in order to provide for the cities expanding in the wake of industrialization. Brick houses with tiled roofs increasingly replaced the picturesque thatch-roofed cottages that had characterized the look of Brabant for centuries and, for van Gogh, were symbolic of home.

To a considerable extent, Gogh's childhood seems to have taken place beyond the four walls of his parent's home. Various and sundry sources mention the boy's daily forays through gardens, fields, meadows, and pine forests. His

Jean-François Millet *The Sower*, 1850, oil on canvas,
42 x 32½ in (106.6 x 82.6 cm), Boston, Museum of Fine Arts

LEAVING HOME

In September 1864, at the age of eleven, Vincent left the country school in Zundert that he had attended since he was seven years old. He would henceforth study far from his home, beginning at the Jan Provily Boarding School in Zevenbergen, where he spent two years. He concluded his formal education after attending the Koenig Willem II state high school in Tilburg for an additional one and a half years. Whether his early departure from home was a lasting, causal factor in van Gogh's melancholy character and the fear of abandonment he so often attested to remains open to debate. It seems at least plausible that his lifelong idealization of home and his childhood could have their origins in this experience. A letter written to Theo twelve years later, in which he insistently described the moment of that departure, gives an idea of how traumatic the separation from his family had been for the eleven-year-old: "It was a fall day, and I stood on the steps of Mr. Provily's school, watching Pa and Mother's cariage as they drove away. I saw the little yellow wagon in the distance on the long road—wet with rain and with sparse trees on both sides— running through the meadows. The gray sky overhead was reflected in the puddles. Around two weeks later I was standing in a corner of the playground when someone came and told me that a man was asking for me; I knew who it was, and a moment later I threw my arms around dad's neck." [82a]

Van Gogh's years of travel began with his time in boarding school. With the exception of his apprenticeship in The Hague, he would never again spend more than two years in one place. There is very little information available today concerning Vincent's time in Zevenbergen and Tilburg. During those years, it is certain that he did not acquire skills that were vitally important to his path in life. But he did learn English, French, and German, and received drawing lessons in Tilburg from the painter Constantijn Huysmans.

It is difficult to ascertain the effect this teacher had on van Gogh's artistic output. There are no letters remaining from Vincent's school days, and the correspondence that has survived does not mention Huysmans. In later life, van Gogh had very little artistic instruction. To a large extent, his rejection of all things academic had a considerable effect on his relationships with teachers. He thus remained largely self-taught, a person who learned by observing and copying works of art, and by expanding his knowledge through literary studies.

Vincent's formal studies ended in March 1868. At the age of fifteen, he returned home to Zundert for a year. This

irrepressible love of nature, which Vincent's letters convey and his oil paintings attest to, undoubtedly harks back to those childhood years. Likewise, Vincent's sympathies with the simple folk apparently had already been awakened at that time. His parents cultivated close contact with the peasants for pastoral reasons. Servants helped to raise the children and handled the daily household chores. Aerssen, a day laborer with a special fondness for little Vincent, took care of the parsonage garden. Years later, long after the family had left Zundert, Vincent wrote to Theo, full of admiration, "What an exhausting life the peasants have in Brabant—Aerssen, for example. Where does their strength come from?" [88]

His fascination with the fruitful life of farmers was expressed later in van Gogh's many portrayals of people sowing, hoeing, digging, and harvesting (illus. p. 12). Vincent saw working the land as the essence of a fulfilling life in tune with nature and the unending process of creation. The biblical image of the sower had special attraction for him. The painting of the same name by Jean-François Millet (illus. above), whom van Gogh considered a role model, can be interpreted as a symbol for the self-image of the parson's son. Vincent copied the image over and over, created his own versions of the motif (illus. opposite), and tried in both his life and his art to be a sower.

The Sower (after Millet), 1890, oil on canvas,
31¾ x 26 in (80.8 x 66 cm), private collection

Jacob van Ruysdael *Landscape with Windmills near Haarlem*, ca. 1650–1652, oil on wood, 13 x 13⅓ in (32 x 34 cm), London, Dulwich Picture Gallery

was to be his final extended stay in his place of birth. His family left there in 1871 because his father was transferred to Helvoirt, about twenty-five miles away. When his course of study ended prematurely, for reasons that are not known, the question of Vincent's professional future apparently created some problems. On August 1, 1869, a decision had been reached: Vincent finally began an apprenticeship as an art dealer at Goupil & Cie in The Hague, a firm headed by Hermanus Gijsbertus Tersteeg, and the company where his Uncle Cent had laid the cornerstone for a successful business career.

IN THE ART TRADE

In The Hague, Vincent got to know a leisurely version of big city life. Compared to pulsing cosmopolitan cities such as Paris and London, later stops on the way to his budding seven-year career in art dealership, the imperial city of the Dutch kings must have seemed rather peaceful, even to the sixteen-year-old. Because it was his mother's place of birth, The Hague was a familiar setting, and he was also warmly received into Tersteeg's home. Very little is actually known about van Gogh's first years of apprenticeship, but it is

Thatched Roofs near Auvers, 1890, oil on canvas,
25½ x 32 in (65 x 81.5 cm), Zurich, Kunsthaus Zürich

possible to imagine from his correspondence with Theo, which began in August 1872 after his brother had visited him in The Hague and the two had become very close, that Vincent's intellectual horizons must have been considerably extended through his work for Goupil, visits to museums, and intensive reading. Vincent appears to have tried to impart his passionate love for art to his younger brother. Vincent was euphoric when his brother finally followed in his footsteps by starting an apprenticeship in the art business at the Brussels office of Goupil in January 1873 and wrote, "Please write to me about all the paintings you see and which ones you think are beautiful." [3]

Goupil dealt mainly in academic art, the conventional salon paintings that were largely in accordance with the tastes of the middle class in the nineteenth century. Although the firm distanced itself from the avant-garde, its program did

encompass works from the Barbizon school, as well as from the Hague school that was inspired by it. Both of these movements played an essential role in the renewal of European landscape painting. A letter to Theo written in January 1874 reveals that Vincent was especially enthusiastic about the exponents of these two, artistic collectives. Millet, Narcisse Virgile Diaz de la Peña, Théodore Rousseau, Constantin Troyon, Jules Dupré, Camille Corot, Charles-François Daubigny (illus. p. 19), Karl Bodmer, Jozef Israëls, and Jan Hendrik Weissenbruch were on a list of painters whom he "especially loved," and "last, but not least, Maris and Mauve." [13] They were all important exponents of these two schools.

The last of these artists was a cousin of Vincent's, Anton Mauve, who supposedly later instructed him in oil painting (illus. p. 13). Since the young van Gogh also met several artists from the Hague school, it may be that his enthusiasm

Edge of a Wood, 1881, charcoal, pen, ink and
white watercolor on paper, 16⅓ x 21½ in (41.6 x 54.8 cm),
Otterlo, Kröller-Müller Museum

▷ **Charles-François Daubigny** *Le Printemps* (Spring), 1857,
oil on canvas, 36½ x 76 in (93 x 193 cm),
Paris, Musée du Louvre

grew even more through these contacts. Nevertheless, Vincent's lifelong veneration of the Barbizon masters, which was fueled by the desire to identify with other artists, to find role models and kindred spirits, was even greater, and they were his chosen idols.

The Barbizon school traced its origins back to the 1840s, when a group of Parisian artists settled in the rural village of Barbizon on the outskirts of the Forest of Fontainebleau, as yet untouched by the Industrial Revolution, in order to commune directly with nature. Despite their completely different views and temperaments, the artists were united by their admiration for seventeenth-century Dutch landscape painting and their rejection of the bourgeois culture that held sway in the capital. Taking British open-air painters such as John Constable, John Crome, and William Turner as models, the artists were drawn to the outdoors. This was a radical approach for an era in which academic conventions dictated

that sketches be done outdoors, if need be, but that real paintings were to be produced in the manageable conditions of the studio; and as far as landscape painting went, it was regarded as an inferior genre.

The Barbizon painters intended to attain a more realistic, yet also more subjective, means of representation. Rather than lofty, heroic landscapes, many of their works highlighted details of a scene, depicting forest glades, stands of trees, or the banks of a stream. It was very important to them to capture the natural lighting conditions and to preserve the moment. These artists met with rejection at first, but beginning in the 1860s they received greater recognition from the Salon de Paris, and as their influence grew open-air painting became increasingly important in Europe. This led to other innovations, including tube oil paints and field easels, which first appeared in the 1850s and 1860s, and to the development of new pigments that allowed, for example, the production of a more intense green. Nineteenth-century technical advances also left their legacy on painting.

It is no wonder that Vincent, an art dealer's apprentice and nature lover, felt attracted to the "intimate landscapes" of these French painters who broke with the idealized classical and romantic representations of nature and prepared the way for impressionism. "Painters comprehend nature, love it, and teach us to see," he wrote to his brother, advising him to "stick to taking lots of walks, loving nature, for this is the right way to better understand art." [13] Even in 1889, at the height of his own creativity, Vincent wrote in a letter to Theo, "I will never forget all those beautiful paintings from the Barbizons, because it is quite improbable that anything better will be done, nor is it necessary" [596].

Vincent was not only partial to painters of the Hague and Barbizon schools, however. He was also unreservedly enthusiastic about the old masters, especially Rembrandt, Jacob van Ruysdael (illus. p. 16), Frans Hals, and other masters of the Dutch golden age, whose works he became acquainted with on visits to the museums in The Hague, the Trippenhuis (predecessor of the Amsterdam Rijksmuseum), and later to the National Gallery in London and the Louvre in Paris.

In the art trade, Vincent laid the foundation for a well of images that would serve to inspire him throughout his entire artistic life, not only in a virtual sense, but also in terms of visual recollection. As an employee of Goupil & Cie, the majority of his earnings did not come from the sale of original paintings, but from dealing in reproductions. As a result, Vincent became passionate about collecting etchings, lithographs, and photographic reproductions. Wherever van Gogh found shelter during the next twenty years, he always decorated his room with pictures by his favorite artists, either for inspiration or to comfort him in his loneliness. His reverance toward certain painters was thus independent of whether he had seen their original works. In fact, Vincent only knew Millet's *Sower* from an etching. In the case of an artist like van Gogh, whose longstanding popularity is based primarily on the highly expressive colors and characteristic style of his oil paintings, this may be surprising. But at the same time, this also indicates just how important the choice of subject matter and "the soul" of a work of art, the spirit in which a picture was created, were to him.

Whenever van Gogh deemed a work "beautiful," the parson's son was making a statement about his beliefs. Even the novice art dealer was not entirely immune to the appeal of salon art, however. On his above-mentioned list of favorite artists was the dean of academic painters, Jean-Léon Gérôme, who was famous for his opulent oriental and classical representations (illus. p. 20). Van Gogh's opinion of Gérôme would soon change, though, in a characteristic way. When Uncle Cor, who was also an art dealer, asked him a few years later if he found Gérôme's *Phryne*, which in its time was widely regarded as the feminine ideal, to be beautiful, Vincent replied that he preferred an ugly woman by Israëls or Millet, or one of Frère's little old women, "For what does a beautiful body like Phryne's mean anyway, since animals also have them, perhaps more so than people. But animals don't have souls, such as those that live in human beings and are painted by Israëls, Millet or Frère." [117] From the

Jean-Léon Gérôme *Pygmalion and Galatea*, 1881,
oil on canvas, 35 x 27 in (88.9 x 68.6 cm), private collection

It may very well be that van Gogh, an avid reader, was pursuing ambitions to be a writer at that time. Efforts at literary excellence are clearly evident in his letters. First and foremost, though, they reveal Vincent's desire to experience the world through the eyes of an artist, that is, to see the heavens "as Ruysdael or Constable paint them." [72] Thus, it becomes apparent that he not only put his encounters with art into words, but increasingly his impressions of nature, as well. Van Gogh had already begun "to depict" landscapes in his letters.

RELIGIOUS BEWILDERMENT

Vincent's secretly nourished intention to become a painter did not prevent him from fulfilling his duties at Goupil satisfactorily. Even a year after his arrival in London, there were no outward signs that van Gogh would veer from his assigned career path, let alone that he would make a radical break with the conventions of middle-class life. After he left Holland in May of 1873, he had spent several seemingly carefree weeks in Paris, and his parents had the impression that Vincent had settled down in England. In truth, however, his spiritual life was losing its equilibrium so far removed from home. In his search for a sense of security,

> *"You must write to me and tell me which painters you like best, both old and new. You must do this, because I am dying to hear it. You simply must go to museums often. It's a good thing for you to get to know the old masters, and if you get the chance, be sure to read about art, especially in art journals, the 'Gazette des Beaux Arts,' etc." [12]*
>
> *Vincent van Gogh, London, November 19, 1873*

very beginning, Vincent understood art as more than the gratification of visual desire; he understood it to be the expression of inner, spiritual beauty.

There is evidence that van Gogh secretly fostered his own artistic aspirations during his apprenticeship at Goupil, as did Theo, it would seem. "I know," Vincent recalled later in a letter to his brother, "that we were both thinking about becoming painters when we were first at G. & Co., you every bit as much as I. But it was such a deep secret that we didn't dare speak of it openly in those days, not even to one another." [347] In fact, Vincent's letters from those years are not only accompanied by sporadic drawings, they also contain written intimations of artistic activity that included phases of great productivity. "I've been drawing again lately," wrote Vincent sometime in the summer of 1847 from London, to which he had been transferred the year before in order to gain experience at the Goupil office there, "but it was nothing special." [17] Very few of his drawings from this early period have survived. Nonetheless, art historians such as Anna Szymanska have emphasized the significance of these youthful works and identified a connection to the Hague and Barbizon schools in several pleasing landscape representations, among other things.

Vincent had fallen in love with Eugénie Loyer, the daughter of his landlady in London, a parson's widow from the south of France. But his courtship bore no fruit, since Eugénie was already engaged to be married. In the months following her rejection, he was plunged into a psychological crisis that affected his professional performance, and thus did not remain hidden from the family. He buried himself in books and shut himself off from the world. Vincent, who had always been a difficult son, became the pastoral couple's "problem child." And it is not without a certain irony

Édouard Dantan *Un coin d'Atelier* (A Corner of the Studio), 1880, oil on canvas, 38¼ x 51¼ in (97.2 x 130.2 cm), private collection

"Country folk, who buy color prints and listen with feeling to a hurdy-gurdy, may deeply sense what is right, and are perhaps more sincere than some big-city types who go to the salon." [592]
Vincent van Gogh to Theo, May 25, 1889

that this development, which would lead to a break with his father some years later, began just as Vincent turned toward religion with growing zeal.

What began in London in 1874 has generally been regarded by van Gogh biographers as the religious bewilderment of the man who would later become a painter. With his characteristic passion, Vincent took refuge in a life of extreme piety and austerity that was dominated by reading the Bible and churchgoing, leaving no more room for the things of this world, such as dealing in art. His letters to Theo give a strange impression of the religious fervor that had gripped Vincent. Efforts to bring him to his senses by means of a change of scenery did not succeed. Beginning in the fall, he was temporarily sent to the Goupil central office in Paris, and permanently transferred there as of May 1875, but he resigned his post on April 1, 1876.

His parents, who had moved once again and were now living in the tiny town of Etten in Brabant, were naturally less than thrilled by what was undoubtedly perceived as the failure of Vincent's respectable career as an art dealer. Even so, they were persuaded to accept his new plans, for he had decided to follow in his father's footsteps and devote the remainder of his life to living out the religious ideal of love for one's neighbors. Thus, van Gogh returned to England in July 1876, where he first worked as an assistant teacher and eventually found a position as an assistant pastor to a Methodist minister in Isleworth near London. In November he gave his first sermon, prepared with great care, and he sent a copy of the manuscript to Theo. The text sheds illuminating light on van Gogh's personality, and at the same time seems to foreshadow the later course of his life. It describes human existence as a constant struggle, comparable to an arduous pilgrimage that, in the certainty of an omnipresent God, must be accepted with humility, but

Three Pairs of Shoes, 1886–1887,
oil on canvas, 19 x 28 in (48.3 x 71.1 cm),
Cambridge, MA, Fogg Art Museum, Harvard University

"The belief that our lives are a pilgrim's journey, that we are
strangers on this earth, is an old one and a good one, but we are
not alone, although it may seem so to us, since our Father is with

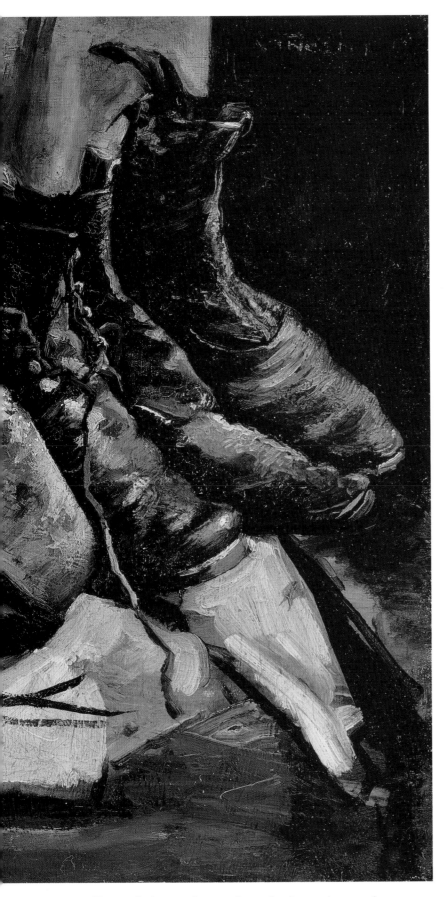

also with a joyful heart. "As sorrowful, but always rejoicing," a passage from second Corinthians 6:10, became Vincent's mission statement at that time. The metaphor of life as a journey would be taken up by van Gogh time and again in his works, especially in the constantly recurring portrayal of his worn out shoes, which could be seen to a certain extent as symbolic self-portraits (illus. pp. 22–23).

Van Gogh now understood the evangelization of the poor to be his calling in life. Still, his engagement in Isleworth remained a one-time episode, and his life remained decidedly unstable. In England, Vincent's (possibly masochistic) tendency toward an ascetic lifestyle and physical exhaustion reached unhealthy levels for the first time. As if he wanted to constantly reassure himself of his own humility, he neglected his own nutrition and set off on forced marches, which he carried out as quasi-symbolic pilgrimages.

Finally, van Gogh's condition deteriorated to such an extent that when he visited his worried parents in Etten over Christmas, they convinced him not to return to Isleworth, but to take a position as a helper in a bookstore in Dordrecht instead. Vincent managed to stay there for all of four months, then went to Amsterdam in May 1877, where he prepared to take up theological studies. This was a concession to his father, who insisted that his son at least acquire the basis for a pastoral occupation. But Vincent soon found the theory to be excess baggage. Having decided to become a lay preacher—a "sower of the word"—he broke off his preliminary studies in July 1878 in order to visit a missionary school near Brussels. After just three months, the reluctant student ended his studies, and in December headed for the Belgian coal region of Borinage, against his father's will and in spite of opposition from the school administration, in order to bring the message of Christ to the miners. Only later, in January 1879, did the missionary commission appoint him to work as a lay preacher in Petit Wasmes, Belgium, for a probationary period of six months.

PREACHER IN A COALFIELD

Van Gogh's famous sojourn in Borinage marks a decisive turning point in his life. A letter he wrote to Theo just before setting off testifies to the fact that Vincent was searching for a fundamental experience there, to live among people whose existence was characterized by hard work, deprivation and lowliness—like the example of the Apostle Paul, who spent three years in Arabia before departing on his missionary journeys. After spending three years in Borinage, van Gogh felt certain that he would have something to say:

Miners, 1880, pencil, chalk, and watercolor on paper,
17⅓ x 21½ in (44 x 55 cm),
Otterlo, Kröller-Müller Museum

▷ *Au Charbonnage Café,* 1878,
pencil and ink, 5⅓ x 5⅔ in (13.8 x 14.3 cm),
Amsterdam, Van Gogh Museum

"I would be better able to master my work and riper for it than I am now." [126]

This is an especially interesting comment, because it can also be understood as an indication that Vincent viewed his work as a preacher in terms of preparation for a career in art. In other words, his interest in art never actually slackened, not even during his years of religious zeal. There is a great deal of evidence in his letters that Vincent, after breaking off his career as an art dealer, dedicated himself time and again to drawing intensively. In addition, he used his stays in Paris, London, Amsterdam, and Brussels not only to deepen his knowledge of the old masters, but also as an opportunity to learn about contemporary artists. So it was that he discovered the landscapes of Fernand Corot and Georges Michel, which he characteristically spoke of in

transcendent terms. "I believe," he wrote to Theo, "that the disciples from Emmaus saw nature as Michel does. Whenever I see one of his paintings, I always think of them." [58]

Van Gogh drew comfort from paintings, just as he did from religion. "What beauty there is in art!" he asserted in the above-mentioned letter from Brussels. "If a person can only recall what he has seen, then he is never empty or lonely, never alone." The presumption that Vincent already had in mind to lend comfort to himself and others via his own artwork some day seems all the more plausible because he added a sketch called *Au Charbonnage Café* (illus. opposite) to the letter. The surviving drawing, which is markedly more expressive than other known early drawings, depicts a simple coalworkers' tavern. The building, above which a crescent moon appears in the sky, almost seems to

have a human quality. With hard, roughly contoured lines and a distorted perspective, it presents a picture of daily life that is shaped by hard work and deprivation—but also creates the impression of peaceful hospitality, security, and dignity. It is significant that van Gogh chose a motif that would hardly have been seen as worthy of painting. This inchoate drawing, in which Vincent's opposition to academic convention already shines through, reveals an interest in the unsightly and the lowly. Likewise, the astoundingly original execution, while admittedly clumsy, seems to con-

sciously flout the imitation of traditional painting. Even if no great meaning were to be ascribed to the sketch, it nevertheless gives an idea of the individual artistic concept that van Gogh had developed prior to the actual beginning of his creative period, thus anticipating the traits of his most important works.

One can hardly imagine that van Gogh realistically anticipated the conditions that awaited him in Borinage. The coalmining region was a showcase for industralization at its most brutal. There Vincent experienced misery, disease, and death at firsthand. He visited the cottages of many workers, descended into the mining tunnels, and witnessed one of the most horrendous mine accidents, which claimed countless lives and resulted in angry worker protests. Van Gogh reacted to the shocking conditions with great sympathy and took action; preaching became secondary. Instead, he supported the families of the miners with all his strength. He cared for the elderly and the sick, read to them from the Bible, gave them his possessions, lived under the most impoverished conditions himself, and again neglected his own outward appearance and health.

Given the radicality with which van Gogh identified himself as an evangelist in the tradition of the earliest Christian missionaries, it is hardly surprising that the church commission failed to extend his contract, even if the justification it gave had to do with his lack of rhetorical competency. Vincent had failed again. But this time the experience of renewed disillusionment had more serious consequences than previously. It not only led to an irreversible break with what van Gogh saw as the bigoted and dogmatic church, but also lastingly shook the foundations of his Christian faith. His relationship with his pastor father did not survive the process unscathed, all the more so because Theodorus showed no sympathy whatever for Vincent's unorthodox and, to him, unbecoming conduct, although he always supported him in his career, as well as financially. Just how dramatically the relationship between father and son deteriorated in those days can be measured by the fact that Theodorus apparently considered declaring Vincent mentally incompetent and having him committed to the psychiatric clinic in Gheel.

Within the family, Vincent was increasingly seen as a troublemaker, an "impossible and suspicious person." [133] For the first time, he hinted at suicide as a way out, but he rebelled instead. His anger was also directed at Theo, who was promoted to the staff of the Goupil central office in Paris, thereby fulfilling the expectations that had once been placed on Vincent. For a period of nine months, from October 1879 to July 1880, the exchange of letters between the brothers came to a standstill.

Hardly anything is known about van Gogh's life during this period. After a short sojourn in Etten, he returned to Cuesmes in Borinage. When Vincent resumed his correspondence with Theo, he reported that he had weathered a "molting period." In fact, Vincent had reached a decision of existential proportions. At the age of twenty-seven, van Gogh had decided to henceforth lead the life of an artist. In the remaining decade before his death, he would paint approximately nine hundred oil paintings.

Rooftops, 1882,
watercolor and gouache on paper,
15⅓ x 22¼ in (39 x 56.5 cm), private collection

"Picture me already sitting in front of my ground floor window at around four in the morning. . . , when people in the little houses all around light a fire to make coffee and the first worker ambles onto the Zimmerplatz. Above the red roof tiles, a covey of white pigeons sails along between the black, smoking chimneys. And behind them, an infinitude of fine, soft green, miles and miles of meadowlands and a gray sky—so still, as peaceful as Corot and van Goyen." [219]

Vincent van Gogh to Theo, July 1882

II. EARLY YEARS AS AN ARTIST (1880–1886)

EARLY YEARS AS AN ARTIST

Sorrow (Sien, pregnant), 1882,
pencil, pen and India ink, 15¼ x 11⅓ in (38.5 x 29 cm),
Walsall, The New Art Gallery Walsall

Pages 28–29
View of the Sea at Scheveningen (detail), 1882,
oil on canvas, 13½ x 20 in (34.5 x 51 cm),
Amsterdam, Van Gogh Museum

AN ART APPRENTICE

During his first months in Borinage, van Gogh had already begun to record the daily life of the miners in sketches, probably in part simply because he needed an outlet to express the shocking experiences he endured there. Though his drawing activity apparently intensified in the fall of 1879, it seems he still needed to make some kind of symbolic gesture to seal his fate as an artist once and for all. In March 1880, Vincent set off on a week-long hike to Courrières, more than forty miles away, to call on Jules Breton, a painter whose representations of country life he admired as he did those of Millet and Israëls. After spending more than a year in industrial and mining areas, during this journey van Gogh again saw his beloved thatched-roof farmhouses and experienced nature. Everywhere along his route he saw figures that incited him to draw or paint—farmers digging or chopping wood, waggoners, and weavers—as he passed through their impoverished villages. Vincent thus felt strengthened in his resolve during this pilgrimage, even though he did not actually meet up with Breton in Courrières.

Back in Borinage, van Gogh worked with single-minded devotion to improve his drawing abilities. The way he methodically proceeded with his autodidactic studies shows that within a few weeks' time he had worked through Charles Bargue's *Cours de Dessin* ("Drawing Course"), one of the most widely disseminated art and exercise books of its day. After that, he undertook Bargue's *Exercises au fusain* ("Exercises in Charcoal Drawing"). He also began to sketch laborers and went about "scribbling down large drawings after Millet" [134] in order to gain experience in drawing figures (illus. p. 31). His very first version of *The Sower*, based on a reproduction by Paul Edmé Le Rat, came about in this way. Unfortunately, like all of his drawings that originated in Borinage, it has been lost.

In October 1880, van Gogh moved to Brussels. He had a thirst to finally visit museums and galleries again, but he was

The Sower (after Millet), 1881,
pen (brown wash), white and green opaque watercolor on paper,
19 x 14⅓ in (48 x 36.5 cm), Amsterdam, Van Gogh Museum

mainly searching for better working conditions. He rented a room and enrolled at the Art Academy to study anatomy and practice perspective drawing. Theo supported him financially and introduced him to the young painter Anton Ritter van Rappard, who shared van Gogh's fondness for realistic art to a great extent and, along with his brother, would become one of Vincent's most important confidants in the years that followed. Apparently strengthened by the exchange with his newfound friend, and also encouraged by the progress he had made, in April 1881 Vincent dared to take what appears to be an amazing step. He reached an agreement with his parents to move in with them in Etten.

While homesickness and the need for reconciliation may have played a role in Vincent's decision, the decisive factor was likely the prospect of free room and board, which promised to offer him greater freedom in choosing materials and models. In addition, Vincent recognized that there would be no chance of sponsorship from his uncle, the art dealer, unless he returned to the family fold. His desire to work outdoors in the open air, in nature, was also a primary factor.

Portrait of Vincent van Gogh, the Artist's Grandfather, 1881, pencil and brown ink, opaque white watercolor, 13 x 9¾ in (33 x 25 cm), private collection

◁ *Woman Praying*, 1882–1883, pencil, coal, brush, gray watercolor, printer's ink, white oil on watercolor paper, 24½ x 15⅔ in (62.4 x 39.8 cm), Otterlo, Kröller-Müller Museum

The time he lived in Etten was a period of ceaseless study for Vincent. He tried his hand at drawings with pencil, pen, and chalk, and began to paint watercolors. Rural scenes and landscapes emerged *en plein air* (in the open air). When the weather was unfavorable, Vincent continued with the *Exercises au fusain* or worked in the style of Millet. He copied Le Rat's etching of *The Sower* a second time, and made portraits of his grandfather (illus. above) and his favorite sister, Wil. Most of these early pictures still look a little stiff, and the precision is not outstanding. An adaptational error that occurred in Vincent's copy of *The Sower* (illus. p. 15) may serve as an example: while Millet's painting shows a flock of crows rising up over the horizon above the farmer's hand, Le Rat's reproduction only vaguely hints at the birds with a few dots in the sky. Van Gogh, apparently intent on faithfully rendering every detail of the little etching to a larger format, changed these dots into corns of grain that the farmer throws up into the air, which is, of course, absurd. The various

The Daughter of Jacob Meyer (after Holbein), 1880–1881,
pencil on paper, 16¾ x 12 in (42.6 x 30.5 cm), Otterlo, Kröller-Müller Museum

▷ Woman Peeling Potatoes (Sien), 1882, pencil and black chalk on paper,
23½ x 14¾ in (59.8 x 37.6 cm), The Hague, Haags Gemeentemuseum

pairs of wooden shoes and other things" [162] in the dark colors of the Dutch masters. Admittedly, these attempts do not yet reveal an individual style.

Perhaps Vincent hoped to find in his cousin not only a teacher, but also an ersatz father figure. With childlike pride, he told Theo that Mauve had admitted that he had falsely taken Vincent for a bore. "I can assure you that Mauve's honest words make me happier than an entire cartload of Jesuit compliments possibly could." [162] The mocking barb against his "Jesuit" father did not come out of the blue, because after a period of superficial calm, conflict in the relationship between Theodorus and his eldest son had escalated anew in the fall of 1881.

The solution to this conflict was Vincent's persistent courtship of his cousin, Kee. He had fallen in love with her in the summer, when she and her son came from Amsterdam to Etten for a visit. At first, the recently widowed pastor's daughter was in all likelihood favorably inclined toward her caring relative, but when he proposed marriage, she brusquely declined. To the family's astonishment, Vincent

Sowers Vincent drew "from nature" at that time typically render sowing more accurately.

In the beginning of his artistic career, Vincent stood in his own way through his search for identity, but his tremendously hard work soon led to positive results. "I no longer stand as helplessly before nature as I once did," he reported to Theo in September 1881 [150]. With growing self-confidence, van Gogh also began to sign his works "Vincent." The consistent withholding of his family name continued the son's distancing from his father in his pictures.

Van Gogh's progress can also undoubtedly be attributed to the counsel of his cousin, Anton Mauve. Vincent insistently sought contact with the renowned Hague artist, who promised his young relative that he would initiate him into "the secrets of the palette." In the fall, van Gogh took quarters in a guesthouse in The Hague for a month in order to receive oil painting instruction from Mauve. Under Mauve's supervision, Vincent's first still lifes emerged with "several

Carpenter's Yard and Laundry, 1882,
pencil, black chalk, pen and brush with black ink, watercolor on paper,
11¼ x 19¼ in (28.5 x 46.8 cm), Otterlo, Kröller-Müller Museum

would not be disuaded. Since Kee refused all contact with him, he traveled unannounced to Amsterdam in November in order to repeat his request at the home of his cousin's parents, whereupon Kee downright fled from him. Vincent took the rejection of his powerful romantic overtures as further proof of the religious hypocrisy and callousness of his blood relations, particularly his parents, who reproached him for not having the means to care for a wife and child. Prior to his religious phase, Vincent had read Jules Michelet's books *L'Amour* and *Les Femmes* with relish. He now immersed himself again in the writings of the anticlerical French historian, and made love his new religion. Since he saw himself as the victim of a pastoral conspiracy, he called his father's authority ever more vehemently into question. And the result was not long in coming. At the end of the year, Vincent left Etten following a quarrel and moved to The Hague.

AT THE FRINGE OF SOCIETY

The departure from Etten was not difficult for Vincent. He gave good reasons for moving to The Hague: the proximity to Mauve, the potential for interaction with Hague artists, and the presence of galleries and museums. After months in the provinces, van Gogh anticipated a fresh impetus, as well as a roomier studio—had Mauve not advised him not to sit too close to his models, because an artist needed greater separation, more distance?

While Vincent was supported by Theo in artistic matters, his brother certainly criticized him over the fight with their father. Theo had distanced himself early on from the Protestantism of his parental home and, in his own faith, had developed pantheistic leanings. Although the two brothers had similar views in this regard, Theo did not have it in him to openly rebel against his father. In the interest of reconciliation, he had tried more than once to pour oil on the troubled waters between Vincent and the hardheaded, willful pastor.

This time around, however, another factor made reconciliation more difficult. After his plans to marry his cousin Kee failed, Vincent decided to look for another woman, and he found her soon thereafter. By December, he told Theo about a woman who was "nothing special." Her name was Clasina Maria Hoornik, and she worked as a prostitute. Vincent did not admit to his brother until six months later that this woman, the mother of a five-year-old daughter and pregnant again at that time (illus. p. 30), was more to

him than just a fleeting acquaintance. Nonetheless, it seems that "Sien" was the one who tipped the scales in favor of van Gogh's departure for The Hague. At the beginning of 1882, he moved into a studio apartment that soon served as a home for the couple. Vincent now had a new family of his own.

The scandalous situation in which van Gogh was living not only shocked the pastor's family when they found

out about the forbidden relationship; it also undoubtedly contributed to Vincent having, contrary to his expectations, little access to artistic circles in the Hague. He found himself increasingly isolated. The relationship between van Gogh and Mauve quickly cooled off. By springtime, Vincent had already left his teacher's studio, also because he refused to work from plaster casts in the academic manner. Tersteeg, his

former boss at Goupil, treated Vincent with nothing less than hostility. Since both of his uncles who worked as art dealers also refused to support their nephew in any way, van Gogh decided to focus entirely on drawing and to take a break from painting for the time being in order to save money.

Vincent had long been enamored of *L'Illustration* and *Graphic*, two journals that featured high-quality prints and

Gustave Courbet *The Calm Sea*, 1869,
oil on canvas, 23⅔ x 28¾ in (60 x 73 cm),
New York, Metropolitan Museum of Art, H. O. Havemeyer Collection

often themes of social realism. Due to his precarious financial situation, at that time he considered working as an illustrator. As a result, a clear interest in graphic elements and striving for contrasts of light and shadow are evident in his drawings from this period. A drawing such as *Woman Praying* (illus. p. 32) not only shows the enormous progress van Gogh had made within a single year, but also testifies to his delight in experimentation. That is why he preferred to use sturdy watercolor paper, on which he combined pencil, ink, and oil pastels, applying printer's black ink thinned with turpentine and using a milky solution as a fixing agent. His techniques were equally unorthodox. He contrasted soft hatching with sharp outlines, brightened up jet-black areas, sometimes even roughened up chalk layers in order to bring shaded areas to life. Van Gogh's seemingly intuitive drawing technique was as amenable to painting methods as his later oil paintings were to various aspects of drawing.

He found most of his models in the homeless shelters of The Hague, but Sien and her young daughter posed for him frequently, as well. His living partner was the model for the lithograph *Sorrow* (illus. p. 30), for example, which belongs to a series of six prints that most clearly express Vincent's ultimately unfulfilled ambitions as an illustrator. It is an unflinching nude of a pregnant woman, drawn from life; its powerful lines and the ornamental structure of the hair and trees seem to anticipate elements of Jugendstil. The representation clearly demonstrates a social consciousness that permeated van Gogh's work at that time, one that would remain present in his later works, but in an altered form.

In addition to drawing human figures, van Gogh also created a series of cityscapes of The Hague, which were commissioned by his Uncle Cor, a one-time courtesy extended by his relative. Beyond that, neither the Amsterdam art dealer nor Uncle Cent supported the aspirations of their nephew to any appreciable degree. The best-known picture in the series is a view from Vincent's first apartment in a street called Schenkweg, entitled *Carpenter's Yard and Laundry* (illus. pp. 34–35). It is an unembellished courtyard scene peopled with working men and women, a yard, a laundry, and a carpenter's workshop, behind which a straight, tree-lined road stretches into the distance through bordering fields and meadows.

This drawing proves that van Gogh had in the meantime mastered complex composition. He had begun to work with a perspective frame the year before, in 1881. When he moved to The Hague, he built an improved version, which soon became an indispensable tool for him. In fact, *Carpenter's Yard and Laundry* already demonstrates an astonishing ability in perspectival representation. The drawing also demonstrates that van Gogh was capable of working through a picture in a controlled way, while combining a number of various techniques in the process—in this case he used pencil, pen, chalk, and brush.

> *"This entire week we've had a lot of wind, storms and rain, and I was in Scheveningen several times to see it. I brought two little sea sketches home with me. There is already some sand in the first one—but the second one, painted while it was really storming and the sea came right up to the dunes, I twice had to scrape off."* [226]
>
> *Vincent van Gogh to Theo, August 1882*

Another interesting aspect is that van Gogh chose private subject matter for the commissioned drawing. Its commonplace contents could hardly have corresponded to the expectations of the client who, in fact, found fault with the entire series due to its lack of market value. Van Gogh always emphasized the unity of life and work, as did his role models. In his choice of subject matter for this commission, van Gogh also lent it a personal, self-reflective dimension, even though it is not typical of his oeuvre. Just as traditional studio representations provide clues as to a painter's artistic concept, this view from the painter's studio window can be interpreted as the artist's view of the world—and of art. In this sense, van Gogh's matter-of-fact picture of the courtyard is evidence of the commitment to realism required by his artistic concept, yet there is still room left for allegorical imagery. Thus, an eye-catching patch of garden occupies a privileged place within the composition, directly below the observer's viewpoint, and that patch is further accented by the artist's signature in the lower left-hand corner of the picture. Only a wheelbarrow and a blooming fruit tree stand in this fence-enclosed area, which becomes a symbol for life's troubles and the hope of a new beginning.

Naturally, this view from the window also gives us information about van Gogh's living situation in The Hague. Apparently his apartment was located on the outskirts of the city in a working-class district, which is surely explained in part by the fact that Theo's regular financial support did not allow for any luxury. But van Gogh's animosity toward wealthy burghers and his sympathy with simple folk would have also played a role in his choice of an abode. Vincent, who once declared himself a "leftist," tried to show solidarity with the underprivileged and to live as an artist. This was clearly evident in his common-law marriage to Sien—which

he defended to Theo and the family as an act of loving one's neighbor—as well as in his use of the poor and the elderly as models in his studio.

Van Gogh's social concerns were also reflected in his literary preferences. Charles Dickens had long been one of his favorite authors. He read Harriet Beecher Stowe's novel *Uncle Tom's Cabin* with great interest. While living in The Hague, Vincent discovered the French naturalist writers, especially Émile Zola, whose works he found intoxicating. Van Gogh's interest in naturalism was in no way due to the need to discover an objective representation of outer reality—it is no coincidence that he kept his distance from the medium of photography, which he felt was cold. Individual expression was paramount to him. "Zola creates, but does not hold up a mirror to things," he stressed to Theo. "That is why his work is so beautiful." [429] Vincent's fascination with Zola also had consequences for his own creative process. Zola's famous definition of naturalistic art as a detail from nature seen through the eyes of the individual is the key to understanding van Gogh's work.

View of the Sea at Scheveningen, 1882, oil on canvas,
13½ x 20 in (34.5 x 51 cm), Amsterdam, Van Gogh Museum

Cottages, 1883, oil on canvas,
14¼ x 21¾ in (36 x 55.5 cm), Amsterdam, Van Gogh Museum

▷ Lumber Sale, 1883, watercolor,
13¼ x 17½ in (33.5 x 44.5 cm), Amsterdam, Van Gogh Museum

BENEATH THE OPEN SKY

Until now, van Gogh's delight in open-air painting had not been particularly visible in his work. As a matter of fact, van Gogh's working conditions in The Hague were largely akin to those of academic artists. He drew almost exclusively in his studio, and even complained to Theo on one occasion about the intense light that streamed into his workroom. That would only change when, at Theo's urging, Vincent again began to dedicate himself to painting. Theo had criticized his brother's drawings as being too dry, which undoubtedly hurt Vincent. But he followed Theo's advice anyway, because he felt obligated to the brother who supported him. So Vincent set off into the countryside to do oil painting without Mauve's guidance and, for the first time, in the outdoors.

Some of these early paintings came into being on the beach at Scheveningen, a suburb of The Hague that the painter Hendrik Willem Mesdag had captured a short time earlier in his famous panorama. Seascapes had long counted among the favorite subjects of landscape painters. They are found in Mauve's work as well as that of other representatives of the Hague school, and also in the oeuvre of the French realist painter Gustave Courbet, whom van Gogh admired.

It is thus not the subject matter of van Gogh's *View of the Sea at Scheveningen* (illus. p. 37) that makes it so interesting, but rather the manner in which he executed the seascape. This oil painting is not exceptional in its compositional refinement or its technical accuracy. Quite the contrary; the picture's true quality is the ruggedness and immediacy with which the simple, horizontally staged composition captures the beach head on from a slightly elevated perspective.

With obvious enthusiasm, Vincent described to Theo the adverse conditions under which the painting was created: "The storm was so fierce I could barely stay on my feet, and I could hardly see anything because of the swirling sand." [226] Van Gogh had to remove sand from the picture numerous times. But the experience of nature also seems to have been inscribed into the painting, which is dominated stylistically by rich earth tones. The raging sea resembles a seemingly uncontrolled color relief in which the crests of the waves stand out brightly like white swells. The gray sky, painted with nearly the same impasto (thick application of paint), is oppressive. In the foreground, one can make out a dune with tall grass tossed around by the storm, hastily executed in a coarse texture. A few brush strokes give shape to a scattered group of people, a horse-drawn cart, and a sailboat.

The color scheme van Gogh relied on here may have corresponded to Anton Mauve's, but the same cannot be said of the painting technique. It is pointless to speculate about role models for van Gogh's impasto style, which is in a rather primitive state in this picture, although he later perfected it in Provence. What we can observe is that even in this early work, even if the circumstances were conducive to it, van Gogh had already distanced himself fundamentally from the fussy, polished painting of the academic tradition that even the majority of The Hague artists had largely adopted. For van Gogh, it was a matter of artistic integrity: "Sometimes, when I am troubled, I have wished I had a bit more cleverness or expertise," he admitted to Theo a couple of weeks before his excursion to the sea. "Yet in thinking it over, I say to myself, 'No. Let me be myself, let me say things that are true with rough, rigorous brush strokes.'" [180]

While the bourgeois concept of art envisioned mastery of the sea motif, this was not van Gogh's intention. Instead, he made his own experience of the storm an integral part of the painting, leaving room for intuition and spontaneity. His spiritual inclination toward nature surely played an important role in this regard. Open-air painting offered van Gogh the chance to commune with nature, like a farmer working in the fields, albeit Vincent's was an aesthetic path, to be sure. If he was walking along romantic pathways in the process, he did not regard this as contradictory to his preference for realism. "Delacroix, Millet, Corot, Dupré, Daubigny, Breton, and thirty more names besides," he brought up to Theo for consideration, "Aren't they the core of painting in this century, and don't they all have their roots in romanticism, even though they have gone beyond romanticism?" [429]

Mauve had tried to correct Vincent's early insecurity by instructing him to keep his distance from his models, and this advice was unquestionably justified. Nevertheless, the beach painting already suggests that van Gogh's particular talent would fully unfold only in close proximity to his subjects, and not at a safe remove. Oil painting emerged as the ideal medium for him, and in the impasto technique

he found a means of expression well-suited his impulsive temperament. "I feel," he explained his first efforts on the beach to Theo, "that elements of color come to me when I paint, things I didn't have before, things of breadth and power." [225]

FAREWELL TO FAMILY LIFE

His promising foray into open-air painting did not change the fact that van Gogh continued to concentrate on drawing, which he still considered to be the area in which he was most talented. At Theo's suggestion, however, he also produced a series of watercolors in The Hague. *The Poor and Money* (illus. right), the most famous of these works, demonstrates Vincent's command of watercolor technique, which he apparently saw as a means of capturing the essence of tangible, everyday scenes, thereby lending them universal validity. In *Lumber Sale* (illus. p. 39), a watercolor completed one year later, "the little people," depicted without individual traits, give the impression of a mass whose hopes seem to be nourished by a variety of diffuse promises, whether it has to do with a state lottery or the words of an auctioneer, who just happens to resemble a pastor.

Despite brief periods of euphoria, van Gogh essentially experienced his sojourn in The Hague as a time of crisis, destitution, and self-doubt. Although Theo actually increased Vincent's subsidies, his financial situation always remained precarious, the more so since Sien had given birth to a baby boy and there were now four mouths to feed in the household. Since Vincent's artistic ideas and lifestyle met with disapproval among the representatives of the bourgeois artistic establishment, all hopes of earning a livelihood with his art were dashed. Yet van Gogh held his ground. "I would rather go for six months without lunch and save money this way than accept ten guilders from Tersteeg, along with his criticisms." [179] This resolve, which he stubbornly professed to his brother, had the same old consequences. As he had so often done before, Vincent neglected his diet and ate poorly, and his physical condition suffered as a result. When he contracted gonorrhea in the summer of 1882, it took him all that much longer to recover from it. Living with Sien, whom he had actually hoped to marry at first, clearly turned out to be increasingly problematic.

Professional and personal problems demoralized Vincent to such a degree that Theo was able to convince him that family life was incompatible with his artistic ambitions. Thus, van Gogh left Sien and her children in October 1883 and turned his back on The Hague in order to settle as a landscape painter in Drenthe, a province in northern Holland. With a heavy heart, he had decided to devote his life almost exclusively to art from that point forward.

The Poor and Money, 1882,
watercolor, 15 x 22½ in (38 x 57 cm),
Amsterdam, Van Gogh Museum

"One has to really think things through before he can comprehend what he's looking at. The expectations and illusions about the lottery may seem rather childish to us, but they are serious indeed when we imagine the misery, on the one hand, and the wasted efforts of the poor wretches, on the other hand, who fool themselves into believing they could possibly find salvation by purchasing a lottery ticket, which they may pay for with the few pennies they manage to scrimp and save by not buying food." [235]

Vincent van Gogh to Theo, July 1882

A PAINTER OF PEASANTS

Van Gogh's selection of Drenthe was no accident, because Van Rappard and Mauve had already worked in the less developed regions of Holland, which were characterized by wide moorlands. Vincent's decision to withdraw to a remote area was also greatly influenced by the example set by Millet. Van Gogh had always been keenly attuned to the spiritual aspect of Millet's peasant paintings. For van Gogh, they revealed God's presence in nature, into which farmers were harmoniously integrated through an unending cycle of work (illus. below). Vincent was equally in awe of the Barbizon artist's personality, and had read Alfred Sensier's biography of the man. Sensier idealized Millet as a modest, deeply religious artist, a seeker of truth who was convinced that in order to represent pristine rural life, a painter had to live as a peasant among peasants. Van Gogh adopted this credo for himself. He wanted to discover his own, personal Barbizon in Drenthe.

The few oil paintings that have survived from van Gogh's tenure in Drenthe are laden with his misguided efforts to imbue the peasant scenes with religious meaning. The painting *Two Women in the Moor* (illus. right) is exemplary. It shows the figures as stooped silhouettes at twilight. Leaning down toward the ground in silent humility, their bodies

▷ *Two Women in the Moor*, 1883,
oil on canvas, 10¾ x 14⅓ in (27.5 x 36.5 cm),
Amsterdam, Van Gogh Museum

Jean-François Millet *The Angelus*, 1857–1859,
oil on canvas, 21¾ x 26 in (55.5 x 66 cm),
Paris, Musée d'Orsay

Weaver Facing Left with Spinning Wheel, 1884,
oil on canvas, 24⅔ x 33¼ in (62.5 x 84.4 cm), Boston, Museum of Fine Arts

crossing the stripe of the glowing horizon, they perform their burdensome daily chores, thereby uniting heaven and earth, as it were. Dawn and dusk, the transitional periods between darkness and light, day and night, become symbolic of infinity. This type of representation is often found in van Gogh's early works, in particular, and the dark color scheme is even more characteristic of his Dutch phase. On the other hand, van Gogh would remain true to the peasant theme throughout his life.

In spite of his initial enthusiasm for his new locale, van Gogh only remained in Drenthe for a mere ten weeks. His frame of mind suffered greatly from the loneliness and dreariness of the moor landscape in autumn, as well as the emotional burden of having left Sien and the children behind. So he returned home to his parent's house one last time, in order to work as a painter of peasants in the little Brabant village of Nuenen, to which the pastor's household had moved in the meantime.

RETURN TO THE FAMILY HOME

Deep within himself, van Gogh may still have hoped that his mother and father would someday understand his passions and feel some solidarity with him. In his letters to Theo, though, Vincent did not seem to harbor any such illusions. He believed that he was nothing more than a "large, shaggy dog" in his parents' eyes, the kind of beast one is unconsciously hesitant to let in the door. "It comes into the parlor with wet feet and is so ragged and wild! It gets in everyone's way. And it barks so loudly. In short, it is a filthy animal." [346]

In communicating with Theo, Vincent judged their father and the "gentlemen of Hague" quite harshly. He accused them of bigotry, and of valuing monetary gain over righteousness. He also gave a bitter account of his youth, which he felt had been "dark, cold, and fruitless." As a result of these experiences, Vincent claimed the artists he venerated—

"Millet, Corot, Daubigny, Breton, Herkomer, Boughton, Jules Dupré, etc., etc."—as his role models. "You must show me the way, and I will more readily follow your examples than those of my father, teachers, and many others." [347]

Vincent's relationship with Theo was also strained at this time. Vincent blamed his brother for the fact that he had abandoned Sien, and he accused Theo of dedicating himself to the business of art, thereby having betrayed art itself. During the weeks Vincent had spent in Drenthe, he had tried to convince his brother to leave Goupil and work together with him as a painter. Since Theo did not take him up on his offer, Vincent indirectly accused him of being responsible for his loneliness and suggested an arrangement that would establish a new basis for their relationship: Theo would send him one hundred guilders per month from now on, and Vincent would send him his pictures in return. Theo gave his consent. From then on the brothers were not only confidants, but also business partners. And so it would remain until Vincent's death.

STUDIES OF WEAVERS

With this agreement, van Gogh entered a new phase of his artistic career. While there had not been any buyers for his paintings previously, he was better able to earn his daily bread as a painter from this point forward. He set up his own studio in his parents' laundry room, and there was no shortage of subject matter for Vincent to paint in Nuenen. While he was still in The Hague, he had written to Theo that he would like to paint the old churchyard on the edge of town, a striking Gothic ruin with a tower, surrounded by an old peasant cemetery and wide fields. In fact, the structure shows up repeatedly in van Gogh's works from the Nuenen period, often as a relatively small background detail in paintings such as *The Parsonage Garden at Nuenen* (illus. pp. 46–47), where it dominates the composition by virtue of its conspicuous shape and positioning. The building became a symbol for Brabant's rural religion, rooted in nature, a leitmotif in van Gogh's Nuenen works.

Weaver Near an Open Window, 1884,
oil on canvas, 26⅔ x 36⅔ in (67.7 x 93.2 cm),
Munich, Bavarian State Art Collections, Neue Pinakothek

The Parsonage Garden at Nuenen, 1884, oil on paper and wood,
9¾ x 10⅔ in (25 x 27 cm), Groningen, Groninger Museum

In January 1884, van Gogh began work on a series of drawings and paintings dedicated to the weavers of Nuenen. During his long hike to Courrières, the weavers' villages had already awakened his interest. And it speaks for van Gogh's social consciousness and nostalgic character that he turned his attention toward a profession that suffered the dire effects of industrialization like no other. Van Gogh felt more than simple solidarity with the weavers, however. As with the peasants in the fields, he was able to identify with them as artisans who carried out their lonely tasks in dark rooms on looms that were often more than a hundred years

old. And while the unemotional realism of his first weaver representations still conveys a certain detachment, this impression visibly recedes over time. The oil painting *Weaver Near an Open Window* (illus. p. 45), dating from July 1884, is perhaps the clearest expression of van Gogh's process of growing closer to his subjects.

In this painting, van Gogh visibly united the environment of the peasants with that of the weavers by having the small window in the weaver's workroom open onto a field, thus placing the man seated at the loom in relation to the woman working in a field behind him. Not only that, van Gogh also

created an analogy between the silent concentration of the craftsman absorbed in his work, and his own work as an artist. The weaver leaning over a length of cloth is reminiscent of a painter before his easel, and the image framed by the window opening from the dusky chamber onto the outside world noticeably resembles a van Gogh's painting of a peasant woman at work and an old churchyard. Thus, the upright, modest, and down-to-earth weaver, a lonely creator like van Gogh himself, became the painter's alter ego.

The extant oil paintings and studies in the weaver series, painted in dark, predominantly earthy tones, were van Gogh's first figures in interior scenes. It is evident that they not only served to capture weavers at work, but also allowed him to experiment with the effects of light, evidently using the chiaroscuro (dark-light contrasts) of Rembrandt and other Old Dutch Masters as benchmarks. Especially in the later pictures in the series, van Gogh was able to capture the complex interplay of light and shadow on the many surfaces of weaving looms in a remarkably skillful way. Apparently, he was more determined than ever to attain the level of craftsmanship in painting that he had previously worked so hard to achieve in drawing.

Still Life with Pots, Jar, and Bottles, 1884,
oil on canvas, 12 x 16¼ in (30.6 x 41 cm), private collection

▷ *Avenue of Poplars in Autumn*, 1884, oil on canvas and wood,
38¾ x 26 in (98.5 x 66 cm), Amsterdam, Van Gogh Museum

EXPERIMENTS WITH COLOR

During the summer of 1884, van Gogh again occupied himself intensively with rural motifs. There was a concrete reason for this: he had gotten to know several amateur painters in nearby Eindhoven and was giving them private instruction, for which he received payment in materials.

One of his students, a wealthy jeweler named Charles Hermanns, commissioned him to design wall paintings for his dining room, which Hermanns then intended to execute himself. The sketches of the designs, a cycle of six pictures that portray peasants working in the fields throughout the seasons, are as poorly preserved as their realization in the patron's home. Nevertheless, Vincent used the drafts for other paintings, such as the peasants in *Planting Potatoes* (illus. p. 12); the two-dimensionality, austerity, and landscape format of that picture are clearly reminiscent of a wall

painting. Significantly, van Gogh avoided monumentalizing the figures, none of the peasants rises up above the horizon. They seem to be entirely at one with the earth as they go about their work.

Van Gogh also took advantage of his employment as a teacher to experiment on his own with a series of still lifes in oil. His students later reported on their teacher's frenzied manner of working, which usually began with one painting in the morning that he finished by noontime, so that he could start a new canvas after a short break.

Relentless experimentation with the effects of color was actually the decisive aspect of van Gogh's work in Nuenen, even if the dark colors may tend to hide that fact. In numerous studies and oil paintings— in contrast to the academic tradition, the dividing line between studies and oil paintings was extremely thin in van Gogh's case—he tried to implement the discoveries that had resulted mainly from his

Head of a Peasant Woman with White Cap, 1885,
oil on canvas, 18½ x 13½ in (47 x 34.5 cm), private collection

▷ *Head of a Peasant Woman with Dark Cap*, 1885,
oil on canvas, 15¼ x 10½ in (38.5 x 26.5 cm),
Paris, Musée d'Orsay

"Anyone who prefers to see peasants looking 'sweet' may stick to his notion. As for me, I am convinced that one gets better results in the long run by painting them coarsely, as they are, rather than by introducing conventional agreeableness . . . In my opinion, it would be wrong to give a painting of peasant life a conventional polish." [404]

Vincent van Gogh to Theo, April 30, 1885

intensive study of Charles Blanc's and Félix Braquemond's theoretical treatises on art. Influenced by their writings, van Gogh's interest in Delacroix's color theories deepened, and the colorist became a leading role model for him.

Delacroix employed targeted, complementary contrasts in his paintings for the purpose of enhancing their coloristic expression. Van Gogh tried to apply these principles to his own work without having had an opportunity to study the works of the French romanticist in greater detail. Van Gogh's lack of familiarity with Delacroix's works, however, led to results in the studies that were not terribly convincing. In point of fact, van Gogh still painted with the earth-tone palette of the Hague masters, and thus with colors that were clearly darker than those Delacroix favored. Under the circumstances, the complementary contrasts could not unfold with the desired impact. Van Gogh would only realize his mistake a year and a half later in Paris.

THE POTATO EATERS

Just how much van Gogh's confidence as a painter had grown became clear when he began preliminary work on *The Potato Eaters* (illus. right), a painting he had apparently conceived as a major work from the outset. Having decided to garner the attention of the art business, Vincent worked tirelessly on portrait studies of peasants (illus. pp. 50–51). Only when his father died unexpectedly on March 26, 1885, was he able to stop for a short while.

In painting numerous "heads of peasants," van Gogh tried out various perspectives and ways of positioning the head, but was chiefly experimenting with effects of light and color. In some of the portraits he seems to have tried to implement Delacroix's ideas by experimenting with the contrasting effects of red and green. He also produced interiors and hand studies in preparation for *The Potato Eaters*, as well as a first draft of the oil painting at the end of February. In April, van Gogh finally dispensed with preparations and, just a few days after his father's burial, began work on the first version of the painting. Yet he was only truly satisfied with a second version—so very pleased, in fact, that many years later he would still describe the picture as his best work.

The painting shows a peasant family of five that has gathered around a small table in their cramped living quarters to eat a simple meal of potatoes with a cup of coffee by the light of an oil lamp. Whereas van Gogh had previously

The Potato Eaters, 1885, oil on canvas,
32¼ x 44¾ in (82 x 114 cm), Amsterdam, Van Gogh Museum

△ *Peasant Woman Digging in Front of Her Cottage*, 1885,
oil on canvas on cardboard, 12⅓ x 16½ in (31.3 x 42 cm),
Chicago, Art Institute of Chicago, Bequest of Dr. John J. Ireland

"If a peasant painting smells of bacon, smoke and potatoes, then good,
that is not unhealthy; if a stall has the odor of dung, fine, that's what stalls
are for; if a field has the smell of ripe corn or potatoes or guano or dung,
that's absolutely healthy, especially for city people." [404]
Vincent van Gogh to Theo, April 30, 1885

▷ *Sheaves of Wheat in a Field*, 1885,
oil on canvas, 15¾ x 11¾ in (40.2 x 30 cm),
Otterlo, Kröller-Müller Museum

Peasant Woman Stooping and Gleaning, 1885,
black chalk on paper, 20¼ x 16⅓ in (51.5 x 41.5 cm),
Essen, Folkwang Museum

concentrated on field work in his peasant representations, from that point on he also recorded household scenes. This theme was nothing new in those days. Nineteenth-century European painting includes numerous representations of peasant meals. What is exceptional about van Gogh's pictures is the unvarnished realism with which van Gogh records this daily ritual.

Even so, van Gogh clearly did not intend that his painting technique would create a true-to-life portrayal of reality. Rather, the faces are crudely overdrawn and look almost like caricatures. Since Vincent had read the physiognomic studies advanced by Johann Kasper Lavater and Franz Joseph Gall, and also admired Honoré Daumier, he wanted to lend a certain animal quality to the peasants' traits, to bring them closer to nature in order to express their essence, uncorrupted by bourgeois culture.

Van Gogh paid great attention to the color arrangement of the picture, which is dominated by dark, earthy tones. The palette emphasizes the organic unity of the scene: the figures appear to be an integral part of their surroundings. Even the faces are hardly emphasized in terms of color. He painted them in the color of a "very dusty potato," Vincent remarked to Theo. "While I was doing that, what has been so rightly said of Millet's peasants came to mind: *'Ses paysans semblent peints avec la terre qu'ils ensemencent.'* (His peasants seem to be painted with the very earth that they sow.)" [405]

Far from creating any kind of romantic image of peasants, the painting shows people who have been shaped by hard work. With stooped bodies, knarled hands, and nearly disfigured faces, they nevertheless exude goodness and contentment. "I have tried very hard," Vincent wrote, "to bring out the idea that these people eating potatoes by the

◁ *Still Life with Bible*, 1885, oil on canvas,
25¾ x 31 in (65.7 x 78.5 cm), Amsterdam, Van Gogh Museum

Still Life with Yellow Straw Hat, 1885, oil on canvas,
14⅓ x 21 in (36.5 x 53.6 cm), Otterlo, Kröller-Müller Museum

light of their lamp have worked the soil with the very same hands they are now putting into the dish. So the picture also suggests manual labor, and that they have earned their daily bread honestly." [404] As such, it would certainly be incorrect to interpret the painting as an indictment of society. For van Gogh, it was not primarily a matter of representing misery, but rather humility and modesty, as well as a family bound together by solidarity and trust, like the one he had certainly wished for himself.

The Potato Eaters occupies a solitary place in van Gogh's oeuvre. With the exception of several still lifes, none of his other works are so clearly oriented toward the chiaroscuro (dark-light painting) and color usage of the Old Dutch Masters, and he would never again put so much effort into a single painting. From a contemporary point of view, it appears almost paradoxical that van Gogh wanted to call attention to himself with a work that was completed in the academic tradition, involving comprehensive study and studio conditions. Just how seriously he took this work can be gauged by the fact that after the first version of the

painting was completed, he prepared a lithograph in order to disseminate the image. Van Rappard's criticism of the painting's coarseness induced van Gogh to break off that friendship. Apparently, van Rappard's stark realism could no longer be reconciled with van Gogh's outlook on art.

The painting, which he sent to Theo in Paris, was not well received for the most part. All the same, the French painter Charles Emmanuel Serret (1824–1900) praised *The Potatoe Eaters*, saying that it might even surpass Millet in expressiveness. It may have been on the basis of this praise that van Gogh decided, in spite of the huge disappointment, to continue working as a peasant painter. In the months that followed, he drew and painted thatch-bedecked cottages, which he called "people's nests" (illus. p. 54), peasants going about their work in the fields (illus. p. 54), and sheaves of grain, which would later become a favorite motif of his in Arles. The August 1885 painting *Sheaves of Wheat in a Field* (illus. p. 55) is a harmonious study in gold and brown tones with a soft beige-bluish sky, which admittedly contains no trace of the expressive coloring of his later works.

LEAVING BRABANT

Van Gogh was not unmoved by the loss of his father, who died of a heart attack. In a still life, he summed up his ever-strained relationship with the family patriarch whom he had once so greatly respected. The painting shows a large, open Bible with a snuffed-out candle beside it (illus. p. 56). In the foreground lies a little book by Zola, *La joie de vivre* ("The Joy of Living"). The oil painting, done "in a single flourish" according to Vincent, is unmistakably in the vanitas still life style of the Old Masters, as reflected in the black background and earth-toned foreground. The Bible and candle symbolize the fleeting nature of earthly life, and at the same time refer to the life and work of the deceased pastor. By contrast, Vincent's deep admiration for the work of the naturalist Zola is shown in the lemon-yellow color of *La joie de vivre*, which stands out within the dark composition, a trouble spot that challenges and provokes the hard truth, just as Vincent did.

Another painting that is counted among Vincent's most expressive works of the Nuenen period can also be understood as a means of dealing with his father's death. It features a diagonal view of the old Nuenen church tower, which was slated for demolition and had already lost its spire (illus. above). The weathered structure, a stone monument to the past, surrounded by simple wooden crosses and encircled by crows, is viewed from slightly below and placed within the picture so that it nearly fills the entire canvas. Allowed to decay, it seems to gradually be returning back to nature. In the ruin, van Gogh recognized "how faith and religion pass away, even though they had been firmly established; how, on the other hand, the life and death of the peasants remains the same, an eternal springing up and fading away, like the grass and flowers that grow in the churchyard. *Les réligions passent, Dieu demeure* ("Religions come and go, God remains") is something Victor Hugo said, and they have also buried him recently." [411]

◁ *The Old Church Tower at Nuenen*, 1885, oil on canvas,
24¾ x 31 in (63 x 79 cm), Amsterdam, Van Gogh Museum

Still Life with Three Birds' Nests, 1885, oil on canvas on wood,
17 x 22½ in (43 x 57 cm), The Hague, Haags Gemeentemuseum

Although Theodorus's death brought an end to the father-son conflict, Vincent was still unable to feel at peace. Tensions between him and his eldest sister, Anna, who criticized him, broke out into a full-blown fight. He thus felt obliged to move into the studio that he had rented the year before from the local Catholic sexton. During the previous summer, van Gogh had already endured yet another ill-fated romance. The neighbor's daughter, Margot Begemann, who was several years older than Vincent, had fallen in love with him and, knowing that a relationship between them was impossible, had unsuccessfully tried to poison herself. Although the families were able to conceal this event from the residents of the village, another scandal the following September had profound consequences for Vincent. He was accused of impregnating a young peasant girl who had modeled for him. As a result, the Catholic priest forbid his parishioners to allow themselves to be painted by the disreputable artist. Without his father's protection, Vincent was practically an outcast in the town.

In the early fall, certainly also as a consequence of this problem, van Gogh turned his attention to painting still lifes, in which he moved forward with his color studies. *Still Life with Yellow Straw Hat* (illus. p. 57) already demonstrates van Gogh's deftness at setting spots of lively, bright colors into a classically dark background without disturbing the harmony of the composition. His various works containing bird's nests, potatoes, and fruit are even more characteristic of that period, and their dark coloring attests to van Gogh's fascination with the Dutch masters of the Golden Age (illus. above). Theo, who had been familiar with the Parisian avante-garde for years, regarded this turn toward the Old Masters with skepticism. He advised his brother to avoid the use of black, which was the custom among the impressionists, who had been the talk of the French capital for years now. Vincent, however, only knew the impressionist painters from hearsay. Just how much the reports about the French painting technique, in which he was not versed, irritated him can be deduced from his letters: "Here in Holland, it is difficult to be clever enough

Autumn Landscape, 1885, oil on canvas on wood,
25⅔ x 33¾ in (65 x 86 cm), Cambridge, Fitzwilliam Museum

▷ *Backyards of Old Houses in Antwerp in the Snow*, 1885, oil on canvas,
17⅓ x 13¼ in (44 x 33.5 cm), Amsterdam, Van Gogh Museum

to understand the true meaning of impressionism," [383] he conceded to Theo, still inwardly convinced that he had found his calling in peasant painting.

In October, Vincent went to the newly reopened Rijksmuseum in Amsterdam with his art students and was freshly inspired by the works of Rembrandt and Hals. But his discussions with Theo gradually began to effect him. The autumn landscapes Vincent painted after his return from Amsterdam have a new lightness. In point of fact, his curiosity about the Parisian art scene had been roused. The idea of moving in with Theo in Paris was often discussed in their letters and it clearly excited him, especially since his situation in Nuenen had worsened dramatically. He sensed that it was time to leave the provinces and confront the avant-garde, but he still did not feel prepared for Paris. When he left Nuenen on foot in December 1885, his goal was to first head for Antwerp. Vincent would never see his Brabant birthplace again.

INTERMEZZO IN ANTWERP

Before he dared to head for Paris, Vincent intended to expand and refine his abilities. Thus, one of the things he did in Antwerp was to join two drawing societies in order to gain experience in nude studies. In fact, he was now prepared to subject himself to academic instruction and enrolled at the Royal Academy of Fine Arts, where he worked from plaster casts with astounding enthusiasm.

The reports of erstwhile fellow students reveal how astonished the professors were by the self-taught student from the Dutch provinces. They were dismayed in equal parts by Vincent's appearance and by his sensational, quick, and unconventional drawing style. In order to achieve greater vibrancy and expression, van Gogh concentrated on reproducing the plasticity of the figures, drawing the bodies with quite coarse hatching and angular lines, almost from the

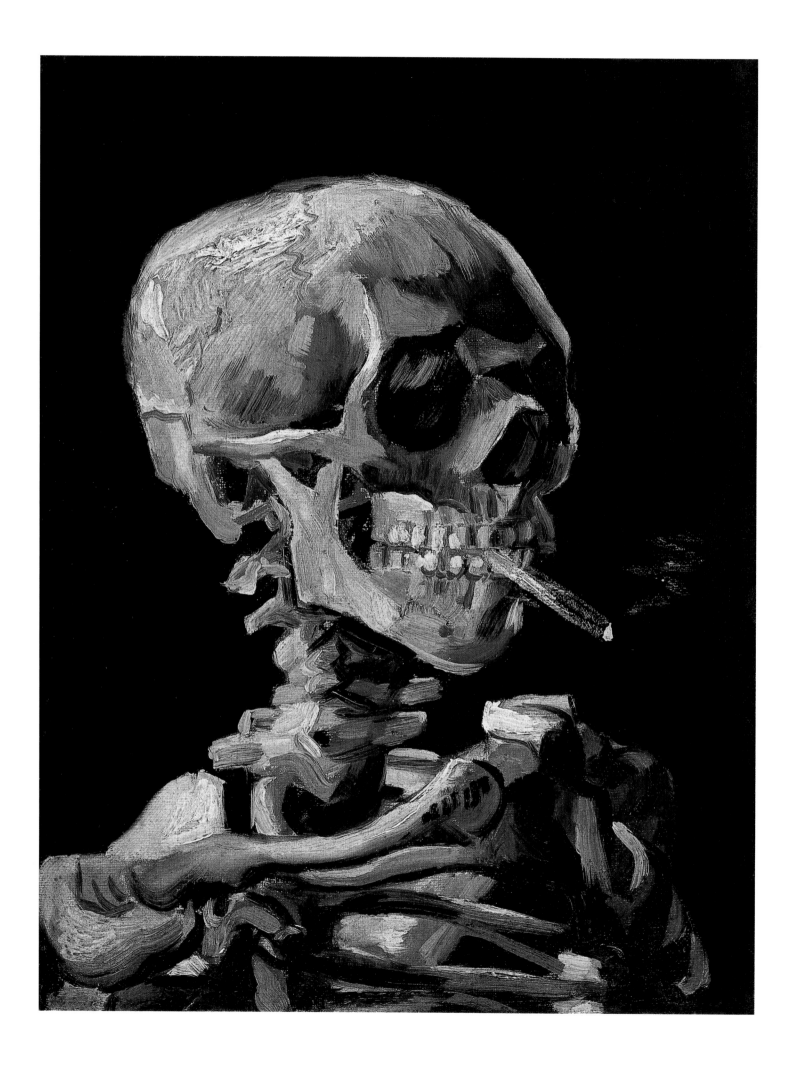

inside out. Students at the academy, on the other hand, were taught to draw figures with clear outlines. These differences, among others, ultimately proved insurmountable, and van Gogh willingly left the academy after two months. However, his brief period of study at the institution has a strange epilogue. Before departing, van Gogh had participated in a competition for entry into the more advanced classes. The results were not available until he was already living in Paris: the professors had demoted him to the beginners class for thirteen- to fifteen-year-olds.

In the birthplace of Peter Paul Rubens, van Gogh's enthusiasm for the great baroque master was awakened. Admittedly, as compared with Rembrandt, he found Rubens to be "shallow and empty" [435] in philosophical and religious matters, but he appreciated the sensuousness and

> *"It is extremely interesting to study Rubens because his technique is so very simple, or better said, it appears to be."*
> *Vincent van Gogh to Theo, January 1886*

Portrait of a Woman with Red Ribbon, 1885,
oil on canvas, 23⅔ x 19¾ in (60 x 50 cm), private collection

vibrancy of his representations of the human body. "Rubens is astounding in his portrayal of everyday pretty women." [444] But what interested van Gogh most was Rubens the colorist, whose influences can be seen in his own portraits. The powerful red and green in *Portrait of a Woman with Red Ribbon* (illus. right), for example, show a less selfconscious handling of color. The surprising eroticism exuded by this vital, powerfully characteristic representation of a simple woman certainly may not have been inspired by Rubens alone. In painting portrait busts, van Gogh was trying to arouse the interest of potential buyers. Once again, his hopes would remain unfulfilled.

Another oil painting van Gogh completed in Antwerp can be seen to some extent as a counterimage to the portrait of a young woman. It shows the portrait bust of a skeleton with a fleetingly painted burning cigarette held between its teeth (illus. opposite). It is rather likely that van Gogh, who was a heavy smoker all his life, painted this as a sarcastic self-portrait. He had also gotten sick again during those months and had lost the majority of his teeth as a result. His heavy workload, poor nutrition, and considerable alcohol consumption may have played a role, but there are also indications that van Gogh had contracted a sexually transmitted disease, possibly

even syphilis. After two years in the countryside, van Gogh apparently wanted to try out the permissive lifestyle of a big-city artist in Antwerp. Several sketches of pleasurable dancing indicate that, at the very least, he did not avoid the nightlife of the harbor city.

Even though van Gogh's intense fascination with Rubens proved to be a temporary phenomenon, he made another discovery during his time in Antwerp that would significantly influence his artwork in the future. In Antwerp Vincent became interested in Japanese color woodcuts, which had been ever more widely disseminated in Europe since the onset of a Japanese trend in the 1850s (see pp. 94 and following). At first, van Gogh's fascination with the dynamic, colorful compositions of the Japanese masters was expressed only in terms of acquiring prints that he used to decorate the walls of his room, as was his wont. A year and a half later, though, Japanese style would be the definitive inspiration for his artwork. But by then, van Gogh had long since reached a new milestone in his unsettled, migratory life as an artist: at the beginning of March 1886, after weeks of inconclusive deliberation, Vincent suddenly decided to board a train and head for Paris. Only upon his arrival did he inform Theo by messenger that he had come earlier than expected. "I will be at the Louvre from midday onward, or even earlier if you like." [459]

Skull with Burning Cigarette, 1885, oil on canvas,
12⅔ x 9⅔ in (32 x 24.5 cm), Amsterdam, Van Gogh Museum

VAN GOGH AND FILM

Big stars have played him, and famous directors have made films about his life and work. Like no other artist, Vincent van Gogh has inspired film makers throughout the world for decades. The movies have contributed significantly to the popularization and continuation of the "Van Gogh myth," to be sure, but at the same time, they have tried to get to the bottom of the legends surrounding him.

Kirk Douglas as Vincent van Gogh in
Vincente Minnelli's *Lust for Life* (USA, 1956)

Motion pictures
Lust For Life (USA, 1956, Vincente Minnelli)
Vincent & Theo (USA, 1990, Robert Altman)
Van Gogh (France, 1991, Maurice Pialat)

Documentary films
Van Gogh (France, 1948, Alain Resnais)
Vincent the Dutchman (England, 1973, Mai Zetterling)
Vincent van Gogh—Der Weg nach Courrières (*The Way to Courrières*)
    (West Germany 1987–1989, Christoph Hübner and Gabriele Voss)

When the first films were shown to a paying audience in the Grand Café in Paris on December 25, 1895, Vincent van Gogh had already been dead for more than five years. He was therefore never able to see moving pictures himself. And it is surely possible that van Gogh would have experienced movies in the same way as he did photography, which he felt was cold and industrial. It was only a matter of time until film and Hollywood would discover van Gogh, of course, even though it was not until 1956 that the dream factory first addressed itself to the dramatic life story of the long-since-legendary artist.

The famous stage director, and "father" of the modern musical, Vincente Minnelli was the one who finally turned Irving Stone's bestselling van Gogh biography, *Lust for Life*, into a movie with Kirk Douglas in the starring role. The main reasons for waiting so long were that the Technicolor process was not able to ensure color accuracy until that time, and the movie cameras were quite immobile, which seriously impeded their use in the wide CinemaScope format. When the film finally reached the theaters, it was a prestigious achievement, the finest in star entertainment: Anthony Quinn shone along- side Douglas in the Oscar-winning role of Paul Gaugin. Furthermore, the film demonstrated the newest technical possibilities of the big studios, which at the time were trying to fend off competition from television by making especially elaborate films.

Today, *Lust for Life* is by far the best-known biographical picture about van Gogh, even if Minnelli's film may not be all that convincing. By today's standards, Kirk Douglas' acting seems overly forced. The action is seldom more than superficial and, in the final analysis, regurgitates the same old anecdotes and clichés. Visually, however, the film is as inspiring as ever. Minnelli was able to spectacularly convey the colors of van Gogh's paintings onto the silver screen, and thereby to bring his works to life in wide, soulful vistas.

Minnelli was not the first movie director to dedicate himself to Vincent's life story, however. In 1948, French director Alain Resnais had already shot *Van Gogh*, an eighteen- minute short film that won an Oscar for best documentary film. Resnais simply used footage of van Gogh's paintings, which he assembled into a continuous picture story and provided with a commentary. This resulted in an internal biography, so to speak, that emanated from the paintings themselves.

Tim Roth as Vincent van Gogh in Robert Altman's *Vincent & Theo*, 1990

Since the film was rendered in black and white, the expressive effect of van Gogh's paintings is derived mainly from the characteristic impasto style that Resnais emphasized, in accordance with the emerging *auteur* (authorship) theory of the day, as the artist's original "signature."

Many *auteur* directors seem to have actually understood van Gogh as a kind of kindred spirit. Akira Kurosawa, for instance, cast American director Martin Scorsese, who is known for his own self-destructive, workaholic drive, in the role of van Gogh in the crow episode for his late work, *Dreams* (1990). Another great American director of independent films, Robert Altman, focused entirely on the decade of van Gogh's career as an artist in *Vincent & Theo* (1990). This many-layered film portrays Vincent on a lonely quest for artistic truth that finally ends in despair, illness, and death, just as Theo's efforts to realize himself through bourgeois art dealership ultimately failed.

Artists' life stories often live on in terms of how they are played by leading actors. Both *Lust for Life* and *Vincent & Theo*, in which Tim Roth personifies van Gogh as a tragic outsider, prove this point, albeit without romanticizing him. The casting of the title role in Maurice Pialat's *Van Gogh*, by contrast, which concentrates on the last two months of the artist's life, demonstrably goes against the grain. Jacques Dutronc, who originally became famous as a musician, bears almost no physical resemblance to Vincent van Gogh and yet plays the artist with a commanding nonchalance that fits wonderfully into Pialat's calm production. Events unfold at length in a leisurely way, capturing the inspiring beauty of the summer landscape in Auvers-sur-Oise with an almost impressionistic lightness.

Pialat, who himself began his career as a painter, presents a van Gogh who is far removed from the myth, a very mortal and thoroughly charming man, but one who is essentially tired of the struggle. Disillusioned by people and life, his suicide seems less like the inevitable ending to a disjointed existence and much more the result of a rising tide of indifference. Clearly, this type of differentiated, true-to-life portrait of the famous painter appeals to a smaller circle of connoisseurs. For a mass audience, the movie industry admittedly presents the old clichés, the most recent example being *Around the World in 80 Days* (2004), in which van Gogh appears as a comical minor character. This once again demonstrates that van Gogh has long since become a pop-culture phenomenon.

III. IN THE ARTISTIC CAPITAL: PARIS (1886–1888)

IN THE ARTISTIC CAPITAL: PARIS

Claude Monet *Impression, Sunrise*, 1873,
oil on canvas, 19 x 24¾ in (48 x 63 cm), Paris, Musée Marmottan

IN THE PRESSURE COOKER OF MODERNITY

Van Gogh's choice of the Louvre as the place to meet his brother already points to an essential motive for Vincent's precipitous departure for Paris. As earlier in Borinage, homesickness for the "birthplace of painting" was one of his main reasons for making an abrupt change of venue. He had not seen an original Delacroix or Millet in years, and he was eager to see his newly won convictions confirmed by standing before his role models' paintings.

Of course, the official reason for Vincent's move was his growing discontent with the Royal Academy of Fine Arts in Antwerp. Back in his Hague period, he had once prophesied that he did not have a long life in front of him, and that he must hurry in order to be able to leave behind a rich, creative body of work. This thought motivated him anew in Antwerp,

▷ *Plaster Statuette of a Female Torso*, 1886, oil on canvas,
16 x 10⅔ in (40.5 x 27 cm), Amsterdam, Van Gogh Museum

Pages 66–67
The Fourteenth of July Celebration in Paris (detail), 1886, oil on canvas,
18½ x 15⅓ in (47 x 39 cm), Winterthur, Villa Flora Collection

probably because of the miserable state of his health. He was afraid of losing time and repeatedly told Theo of his desire to work in Fernand Cormon's studio in Paris. His brother had told Vincent about the historical painter who, despite his own academic style, was known for allowing his students a relatively free hand.

The prospect of living with Theo may have played a role in Vincent's decision. In Antwerp, it became clear to him that the alienation from his mother and his two eldest sisters was irreversible. In his loneliness, he longed to be near his brother. Theo agreed to have Vincent share his home, but wanted to wait until June, when a larger apartment would become available at Rue Lepic 54 in Montmartre. But Vincent did not allow him that time, and so the brothers spent three months together in a cramped, two-room apartment. Very little information exists concerning their everyday life, which surely could not have been tension free, and the same is true of the nearly two years that van Gogh spent in Paris. Sharing an apartment made brotherly correspondence unnecessary.

Ten years had passed since van Gogh's last stay in Paris. The face of this city of millions had changed remarkably in the meantime; the Industrial Age had been ushered in at top speed. While suburbs and factories shot up on erstwhile agricultural land, the rich bourgeoisie expressed its growing economic power in the grandeur of the increasingly impressive buildings along the boulevards. The feverish development in the French capital reached its peak in the year after Vincent's arrival, when construction began on the Eiffel Tower. This structure, more than any other, reflected the great nation's need for recognition as a driving force of modernity. It would be dedicated on the occasion of the 1889 World Exhibition.

Still, first and foremost Paris held the distinction of being the unchallenged artistic capital of the world. Since Vincent had last been there, groundbreaking events had also taken place in the business of art. The time-honored Salon de Paris was still the annual highpoint of cultural life because for the public at large, fine academic painting served as a palpable sign of artistic quality. Since the first Impressionist Exhibit in 1874, however, avant-garde art had powerfully entered into public consciousness, along with an entirely new concept of art.

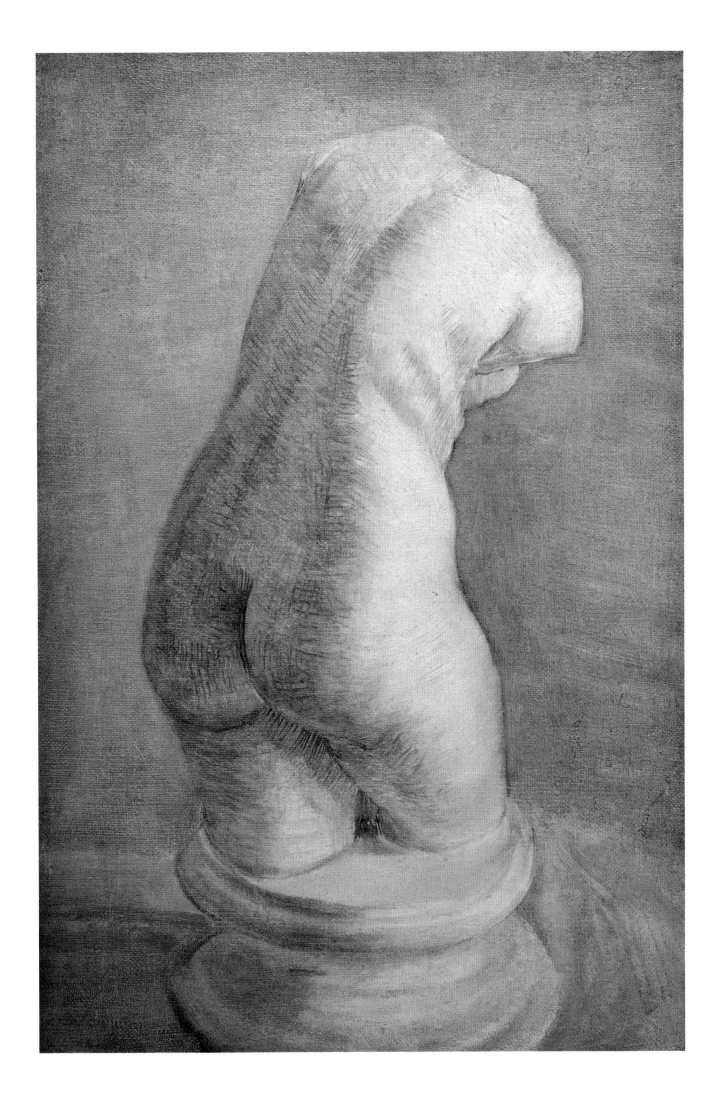

Georges Seurat *The Eiffel Tower*, c. 1889, oil on canvas, 9½ x 6 in (24.1 x 15.2 cm), San Francisco, Fine Arts Museum of San Francisco

Prior to that time, impressionism had been the most radical attempt to create a modern, up-to-date aesthetic and to free painting from the constraints of its academic corset. To begin with, it was provocative of the impressionists to reject "great" themes at a time when historic painting was considered the most important of all genres, and to instead draw their motifs from everyday life, their immediate surroundings, and nature. Yet what turned out to be seminal was impressionism's break with illusionist convention. Rather than bringing objective reality to life, painters reproduced natural sights, capturing the subjectively experienced moment. Picking up on the approach of the Barbizon plein air painters, they made allowance for the changing effects of light and color. But their concepts and techniques went far beyond the "intimate landscapes" of their predecessors: the lighter palette of primary colors, sketch-like designs, and the finely speckled or characteristically dotted style that dissolved outlines. In their paintings, impressionists ultimately proclaimed the freedom of the artistic subject.

The impressionist movement showed signs of disintegration in 1886, but a number of its protagonists, including Claude Monet, Auguste Renoir, and other painters of the Grand Boulevard scene, had gained a place for themselves in the art marketplace. And while plein air painting was slowly but surely gaining a foothold, the early post-impressionist movement was creating a sensation. Pointillists and divisionists were systematizing the impressionist technique of dotting based on scientific discoveries (illus. left). Modernism had taken root and would henceforth continually cause cracks in the foundation of the ossified academic art establishment.

At best, Van Gogh had only a vague idea of the innovations the impressionists had introduced in the discipline of painting. In previous years, he had seen pictures only by the great leader of the movement, Édouard Manet. That did not stop him, however, from concluding that it was not Manet, but rather Millet, who as a modern painter had "opened up new horizons for many" [355]—which was undoubtedly true in van Gogh's case. When Vincent arrived in Paris in the spring of 1886, the Barbizon Masters were still the *non plus ultra* of modernity. But within two years' time, that would change dramatically.

In 1886, there were three important exhibitions in Paris alone that may well have emphatically shaken van Gogh's artistic conceptions. The eighth and final Impressionist Exhibition took place in May, at which Edgar Degas and Paul Gauguin, whose paintings were still characteristically impressionistic, were represented alongside Camille Pissarro, Georges Seurat, and Paul Signac, all three of whom exhibited pointillist works. Seurat introduced his painting *A Sunday Afternoon on the Island of La Grande Jatte*, the quintessential programmatic work of the pointillist style. One month later, Monet and Renoir presented their latest works at the Fifth International Exposition of Painting and Sculpture, after which Pissarro, Seurat, and Signac again exhibited additional post-impressionist works at the Second Independant Salon in late summer.

Van Gogh soon traveled in Parisian artistic circles. He met Signac, Seurat, Pissarro, and his son Lucien through Theo, who as head of the Goupil office on Boulevard Montmartre was always looking for ways to support burgeoning art forms. At Cormon's studio, where Vincent presumably studied during the spring and summer of 1886, he befriended Henri de Toulouse-Lautrec, Louis Anquetin, John Russell and Émile Bernard, who were all taking courses there, as well. Gauguin was also among his circle of acquaintances. And van Gogh met other important contemporary artists at Julien Tanguy's art supply store. Tanguy was an art enthusiast, fondly known as "Père" Tanguy because of his support of the avant-

View of Paris from Vincent's Room in the Rue Lepic, 1887,
oil on canvas, 18 x 15 in (46 x 38.2 cm), private collection

*"There is a lot to see here—Delacroix,
for example, just to name a single master.
In Antwerp, I didn't even know
who the impressionists were. Now I have
seen them, and although I don't belong to
their club, I do admire certain impressionist
paintings very much—Degas'
nudes—Claude Monet's landscapes."* [459a]

*Vincent van Gogh to fellow student
in Antwerp, Horace Mann Levens,
Paris, August/October 1886*

garde. Van Gogh experienced Paris as the pressure cooker of modern art. The multitude of impressions and stimuli that crowded in on him could not help but have an effect on his own work. So it was that his radical transformation from an unconventional yet ultimately traditional painter to an avant-garde artist occurred through the approximately two hundred oil paintings that van Gogh completed while living in Paris.

SELF-PORTRAITS

During his time in Paris, Vincent began to paint self-portraits on a regular basis. Indeed, twenty-nine of his thirty-five self-portraits can be traced to this period of creativity. There are a number of explanations as to why he focused on this particular subject matter. At first, the self-portraits served as an inexpensive way for Vincent to experiment, offering him the opportunity to play with and explore the effects of color and painting techniques without having to pay models. It is also possible that Vincent not only regarded portrait painting as a means of self-instruction, but also as a possible path to earning money; by making self-portraits he may have wanted to draw attention to himself as a portraitist.

Moreover, it is also entirely plausible that a mentally unstable artist such as van Gogh used the self-portraits as a means to analyze himself, to practice a kind of self-therapy. The pictures often seem to provide direct insight into the painter's state of mind. They have thus shed considerable light on the psychological interpretation of van Gogh's entire artistic output. The Parisian self-portraits clearly reveal the first signs of expressionism, which van Gogh would refine, inimitably, in Arles and Saint-Rémy.

Last but not least, van Gogh positions himself and reflects upon himself as an artist in the self-portraits. Most notably, the two self-portraits he produced in the studio (at the easel) at the beginning and the end of his Paris period must be understood as programmatic works, and they clearly show the astounding artistic development van Gogh was going through at that time. The first of these works (illus. p. 74) shows the painter at an easel in a blue-green smock, wearing a dark felt hat. Holding the palette, he fixes his gaze on the

Fishing in Spring, 1887,
oil on canvas, 20 x 23⅔ in (50.5 x 60 cm),
Chicago, Art Institute of Chicago, gift of Charles Deering McCormick,
Brooks McCormick, and Roger McCormick

of the artist and vice versa, and turns the act of painting into a sort of ironic mind game. We actually know what the artist is looking at, namely his own mirror image, which is realistically expressed in the first of these two self-portraits. But at the same time, we are denied the opportunity to look at his canvas. Thus, our attention turns to the creative act itself, that is, to the question of how the artist appropriates reality and how he implements the pictorial motif.

In the process, through ingenious staging of the lighting, van Gogh manages to direct the observer's attention to the problem of the color arrangement. Light falls sideways in a way that emphasizes the palette, the shoulders, and cheeks, as well as the picture frame, producing a direct connection between the colored oil paints on the palette and, above all, the colors of the artist's orange-red beard and blue clothing. In his self-portrait, Vincent thus announces himself to be a colorist. He produces colorful accents by using complementary contrasts in the style of Delacroix— orange and blue—yet the "Dutch" tones remain definitive. Pure red, for example, only shines through occasionally on the dark palette; in the picture itself, it is only found blended in.

Comparing the later self-portrait before the easel (illus. p. 75) with the first one, a wondrous metamorphosis becomes clearly apparent. Although the subjects are almost identical, hardly any similarities in execution can be discerned. In the second picture, completed just prior to his departure from Paris, van Gogh seems to want to distill the experiences of the past year and a half into a single image. Even though the composition of the two self-portraits is fairly uniform, the later picture looks far more dynamic simply because of the emphasis on diagonal lines. Even more important are the fundamentally changed brush strokes and entirely new color scheme, which reveal his distinctive utilization of impressionist techniques.

The dark color scheme has disappeared. Pure colors gleam on the bright palette in the artist's hand, and in the self-portrait they are placed side by side in short brush strokes and freely executed dots that draw from the impressionist manner, albeit the material is applied much more forcefully. Complementary colors are everywhere: the blue of the jacket with orange highlights, the red of the lips and eyebrows with green contrasts. The colors of the room itself are almost entirely subdued, and a free play of colors seems to dominate. Only in the light gray background do the bright colors recede, and even though the background has a powerfully textured characteristic style, the picture hardly gives the impression of spatial depth.

observer with a serious expression, but his face is hidden in shadow. Van Gogh presents himself here unmistakably as an artist in the tradition of the Old Dutch Masters. In its composition, coarse style, dark colors, and chiaroscuro effects, the painting is probably intentionally reminiscent of Rembrandt's self-portrait at the easel, which van Gogh had certainly seen at the Louvre.

What is interesting about this type of self-portrait is that in a certain way it makes the observer into a mirror image

Self-Portrait with Dark Felt Hat at the Easel, 1886, oil on canvas,
18 x 14¾ in (45.5 x 37.5 cm), Amsterdam, Van Gogh Museum

▷ *Self-Portrait as an Artist,* 1888, oil on canvas,
25¾ x 21¾ in (65.5 x 55.5 cm), Amsterdam, Van Gogh Museum

Adolphe Joseph Monticelli *Vase with Flowers*, 1875,
oil on wood, 25½ x 17¾ in (65 x 45 cm), private collection

▷ *Vase with Gladiolas and Carnations*, 1886,
oil on canvas, 35¾ x 20 in (91 x 50.5 cm), Zurich, Kunsthaus Zürich

In this self-portrait, van Gogh has left behind both mimicry and the impressionistic capturing of a fleeting moment. His coloration and style are expressive, allowing objective reality and inner experience to meld. It appears the painter's glance is directed within and without in equal measure. Striking, as well, is that the fall of light on the side is just vaguely noticeable. Only above the face is there a clear shadow, giving the impression that the artist might be engulfed by the darkness of his own work. Apparently van Gogh painted himself as an artist who is fatefully bound to his own creativity. "You will say," he said to his sister Wil about the self-portrait, "that it looks a bit like the face—of death" [W4]. Interestingly, Vincent emphasized that he had painted the portrait "in the mirror." "Of course, I look different now, since I have neither hair nor a beard, because I shave them smooth. And my facial color has gone from gray-green pink to grayish orange." Vincent humorously conveys here that his art does not spring from fantasy, but always remains tied to reality.

A DUTCHMAN IN PARIS

The transformation of van Gogh's artwork that emerged in light of the two self-portraits did not take place in fits and starts. Vincent's first encounters with impressionist paintings did not particularly delight him, nor were they immediately reflected in his work. Van Gogh apparently had enough self-confidence to initially stand by his own artistic concepts.

In the summer of 1886, he turned to painting floral still lifes, a favorite subject of the French painter Adolphe Monticelli (illus. above left), who had died in June of that year and whom van Gogh greatly admired. Van Gogh saw

Bowl with Peonies and Roses, 1886, oil on canvas,
23½ x 28½ in (59.8 x 72.5 cm), Otterlo, Kröller-Müller Museum

still lifes primarily as exercises. In them, he not only tried to reproduce Monticelli's impasto style, but he also experimented with contrasts in order to increase the intensity of the colors in his work. Within the space of a few months, van Gogh produced countless paintings and oil studies of brightly colored bouquets that document his increasing confidence as a colorist (illus. above, opposite). With his floral still lifes, he found noteworthy recognition for the first time. A Parisian art dealer took several paintings on commission, and van Gogh also traded still lifes for works by other artists. Even his Uncle Cent acquired one of his pictures in exchange for two watercolors. Vincent apparently wanted to support Theo's plan to become a financially independent art dealer by making this contribution toward building up a collection. Although his brother's plan never materialized, Vincent enthusiastically continued to trade pictures from then on.

The powerful colors of van Gogh's floral still lifes had little effect on his cityscapes painted during the same period. Admittedly, he sometimes tried to include colorful accents, and his earliest Parisian plein air paintings do radiate greater freshness than his earlier works. But his oil study named for Bastille Day (*The Fourteenth of July Celebration in Paris*, illus. p. 78; detail, pp. 66–67) is the earliest work to reflect his desire to capture big-city reality in full color and to thereby open himself to the tide of modern art. Eight years earlier, a similar celebration with flags had also inspired Monet to paint *La Rue Montorgueil*.

Late in the summer of 1886, van Gogh painted *View of Paris from Montmartre* (illus. pp. 78–79) in the old, familiar Dutch color scheme. The view of a seemingly endless gray sea of houses with roofs that shimmer in matte browns and reds seems to express not Vincent's fascination with the

The Fourteenth of July Celebration in Paris, 1886,
oil on canvas, 17⅓ x 15⅓ in (44 x 39 cm), private collection

▷ *View of Paris from Montmartre,* 1886,
oil on canvas, 15¼ x 24¼ in (38.5 x 61.5 cm),
Basel, Kunstmuseum Basel

metropolis, but rather his alienation from it. It seems the painter of peasants only gradually came to terms with the landscape of the city. He mainly found his plein air subject matter in areas that reminded him more of his Brabant birthplace: the favorite excursion destination of Montmartre with its *Moulin de la Galette* (Galette windmill), surrounding garden locales, and the north side of the "Butte," which still had a rural feeling. The search for traces of impressionism in *The Hill of Montmartre with Quarry* (illus. p. 81), painted in the autumn, is futile. Instead, van Gogh once again expressed his reverence for his old favorites, Ruysdael and the Barbizon masters.

THE IMPRESSIONIST PHASE

Stronger impressionist echoes first appear in van Gogh's work during the winter of 1886–1887. *Self-Portrait with Grey Felt Hat* (illus. p. 82), for instance, presumably painted around the turn of the year, visibly uses impressionist painting style and dotting technique, but does not exhibit its brighter palette. The city attire that Vincent wore for this picture could signify that he was gradually becoming accustomed to the bohemian lifestyle. In the literature, there are certainly various speculations that van Gogh may have wanted to thus present himself to collectors as a portraitist. Two other representative self-portraits that date from the spring of 1887 would seem to confirm this.

But these two paintings, in which the painter presents himself in an unusually dandified way (illus. p. 83), are especially interesting because they show an entirely new color scheme within van Gogh's oeuvre. In place of the dark colors of his early works, he avails himself of the fresh, light colors of the Parisian avant-garde. Light blue, intense green, red, and orange replace the earthy tones that had characterized van Gogh's oil paintings ever since his apprenticeship with Mauve. The fresh palette and impressionistic style are also found in his cityscapes from that spring. In *View of Paris from Vincent's Room in the Rue Lepic* (illus. p. 71) and *Vegetable Gardens at Montmartre* (illus. pp. 84–85), which was painted at about the same time, complementary contrasts fully unfold through the use of primary colors. Black is almost entirely

Le Moulin de la Galette, 1886, oil on canvas,
15 x 18⅓ in (38 x 46.5 cm), Berlin, Neue Nationalgalerie,
Staatliche Museen zu Berlin—Preußischer Kulturbesitz

▷ *The Hill of Montmartre with Quarry*, 1886,
oil on canvas, 22¼ x 24⅔ in (56.2 x 62.5 cm)
Amsterdam, Van Gogh Museum

absent; even the shading is painted in full color. The thin color application is characteristic of impressionist painters, but seems atypical for van Gogh, who tended toward impasto application. Under the influence of the impressionists, his distinctive style seems to have become temporarily blurred. He viewed himself as a perpetually searching artist, and as a result, tried out new approaches in his own work, less out of deep conviction than for the purpose of study and learning.

The impressionist tendencies in his work must certainly have also been the result of deepening friendships. During the winter, Vincent's relationship with Theo was temporarily strained when his brother became ill. Presumably for this reason, Vincent sought the company of other painters. He formed a painters' clique with Lautrec, Anquetin, and

Bernard that went by the name of "Petit Boulevard," an ironic allusion to the established impressionists of the Grand Boulevard. In 1887 he produced two group exhibitions with them, the first in the Café du Tambourin on Boulevard de Clichy, which had for a time been a favorite locale for this circle of friends. The owner of the café, Agostina Segatori, was a former artist's model, and van Gogh allegedly had a short liaison with her. Three female nudes from that period suggest this. The second exhibition was held in a local eating establishment on Avenue de Clichy. Neither exhibition had a large impact. Nevertheless, Vincent's work was seen publicly in Paris for the first time.

Beginning in the spring, Vincent regularly traveled to Asnières-sur-Seine, a Parisian suburb that had retained its

small-town character (illus. pp. 72–73) and was among the favorite spots where the impressionists painted. He was often accompanied on his sojourns by Émile Bernard, whose parents lived there. The famous photograph of the pair was taken on one such painting excursion; in it, Vincent is seen sitting at a table with his back to the camera (illus. foldout).

Van Gogh also worked repeatedly with Signac in Asnières. Vincent's forays into the pointillist technique in the spring and summer of 1887 were undoubtedly due to the friendship between van Gogh and the young painter, as well as his contact with Seurat, who was not much older. In the course of the year, Vincent also organized an exhibit with these two fellow artists, this time in the foyer of the Théâtre Libre, a demonstrative gesture of solidarity among artists who would

always remain close to van Gogh's heart, even though Bernard, in particular, would vehemently reject pointillism.

Seurat and Signac had forcefully advanced the dotted technique of the impressionists while also systematically applying new scientific discoveries concerning the physiology of the human eye. They placed color on the canvas in fine dots according to a precise plan, using only primary colors. For this reason, the full effect of their compositions was only revealed when they were viewed at a distance, because the dotted structure of the picture then dissolved optically through the layering of colors. Given the precision that this method required, those works that are narrowly defined as pointillist had to be painted in the studio, while plein air pictures should be considered studies. Pointillist paintings

Self-Portrait with Grey Felt Hat, 1887, oil on canvas,
16¼ x 12⅔ in (41 x 32 cm), Amsterdam, Stedelijk Museum

▷ *Self-Portrait with Grey Felt Hat,* 1887, oil on canvas,
7½ x 5½ in (19 x 14 cm), Amsterdam, Van Gogh Museum

Vegetable Gardens at Montmartre, 1887, oil on canvas,
17⅔ x 31¾ in (44.8 x 81 cm), Amsterdam, Van Gogh Museum

Fritillaries in a Copper Vase, 1887, oil on canvas,
29 x 23¾ in (73.5 x 60.5 cm), Paris, Musée d'Orsay

▷ *Trees and Undergrowth,* 1887, oil on canvas,
18⅓ x 21¾ in (46.5 x 55.5 cm), Amsterdam, Van Gogh Museum

Couples in the Voyer d'Argenson Park in Asnières, 1887,
oil on canvas, 29½ x 44⅓ in (75 x 112.5 cm), Amsterdam, Van Gogh Museum

Bridge Across the Seine at Asnières, 1887,
oil on canvas, 20½ x 25½ in (52 x 65 cm), private collection

▷ *Wheat Field with a Lark*, 1887, oil on canvas,
21¼ x 25¾ in (54 x 65.5 cm), Amsterdam, Van Gogh Museum

therefore lack that feeling of spontaneity, that atmosphere of an immediate natural impression, that characterizes impressionist art. For this reason, pointillism ultimately represents an overcoming of impressionism, rather than a further development of it. That an impulsive painter like van Gogh would try his hand at a technique as highly controlled as pointillism is rather astonishing. In truth, a more rigorous utilization of the style appears in only a few of his works,

such as *Couples in the Voyer d'Argenson Park in Asnières* (illus. p. 87). The careful composition and refined execution, as well as an unusually large format for van Gogh, lead one to assume that he undertook the final work on the picture in the studio, although he preferred to work with his subject directly in front of him. What is more characteristic of van Gogh's style is that he did not strictly apply the technique and, as in the case of *Vegetable Gardens at Montmartre* (illus. pp. 84–85), he interspersed the dotted technique with short, thick brush strokes.

This brief pointillist episode in van Gogh's oeuvre is but one typical example of his fundamental openness to strange new ideas, which, if they interested him, he would quite faithfully adopt in order to eventually incorporate them into his own original and completely unique style—or to discard them. The lasting merit of his impressionistic and

Page 90
Agostina Segatori Sitting in the Café du Tambourin, 1887,
oil on canvas, 21¾ x 18⅓ in (55.5 x 46.5 cm),
Amsterdam, Van Gogh Museum

Page 91
Self-Portrait, 1887, oil on canvas,
17⅓ x 13¾ in (44 x 35 cm), Paris, Musée d'Orsay

pointillist efforts lay in his use of color as a largely autonomous means of expression from that time on. In addition, he developed great flexibility and self-confidence in the use of a wide variety of techniques. An oil painting such as *Bridge Across the Seine at Asnières* (illus. opposite), which departs from the actual colors of the place almost entirely, suggests how freeing this approach to color was. All the same, van Gogh never considered himself a true member of the impressionist "club."

GETTING AWAY FROM THE METROPOLIS

Vincent apparently did not share the fascination of many impressionists with the energy and commotion of daily life in the modern metropolis. His Parisian works reveal neither a particular soft spot for big-city life nor for the achievements of technological progress. The tender portrait of *Agostina Segatori Sitting in the Café du Tambourin* (illus. p. 90), a typical theme among bohemian artists of the day, counts as one of the few exceptions. Van Gogh was anything but the famous *peintre de la vie moderne* ("painter of modern life") that Charles Baudelaire had once proclaimed. While the spiritual aspect of his art faded into the background while he was living in Paris, and his identification with Millet may have temporarily waned at that time, still van Gogh ultimately remained true to his understanding of himself as a peasant painter, even in the metropolis. Remarkably often he sought out his subject matter on the outskirts of Paris. In *Outskirts of Paris: Road with Peasant Shouldering a Spade* (1887), he apparently even placed himself in the picture as the figure of a man with a red beard and a straw hat. Self-representations of this kind would later become a fixed, iconographic component of his works.

Nude Woman Reclining, Seen from the Back, 1887,
oil on canvas, 9½ x 16¼ in (24 x 41 cm), private collection

"Above all, I wish I were less of a burden to you. And that may not be impossible from now on, for I hope to make progress so that you'll be able to show my things without having second thoughts, without having to compromise yourself. And then I will withdraw to someplace in the south, where I won't have to see so many painters who are disgusting to me as human beings." [462]

Vincent van Gogh to Theo, summer 1887

In some of van Gogh's Parisian pictures, the wildly growing city, rapidly expanding into the country around it, seems to take on almost menacing traits. An example of this is *Outskirts of Paris near Montmartre* (illus. right). The painting is as much an indication of Vincent's discomfort with progressive industrialization, however, as it is a sign that his mood had begun to darken. A series of gloomy self-portraits from the summer of 1887 (illus. p. 91) are indications that he felt increasingly ill at ease in Paris. In fact, he was disturbed by his dependence on Theo, the lack of recognition for his art, and the competitive behavior of artists toward one another. His brother's plans to marry also made Vincent all the more painfully aware of his own personal misery.

Once again, van Gogh experienced a growing desire for change. He longed to be in the countryside. This time it was not his birthplace that lured him, but rather the powerful, bright colors of the south of France. A year earlier, just months after his arrival in Paris, he had toyed with the idea of going to southern France. This idea now combined with his intensifying interest in Japanese woodcuts, which had been fueled by his focused, systematic reading ever since Antwerp. For Vincent, Japan became the paragon of a southern paradise, a utopian land of colors where artists worked together collaboratively and showed their respect for one another by exchanging pictures.

Outskirts of Paris near Montmartre, 1887,
pastel and gouache on green paper,
15½ x 21 in (39.5 x 53.5 cm),
Amsterdam, Stedelijk Museum

"I've long found it fascinating that Japanese artists so often exchanged pictures with one another. This proves that they valued one another, supported each other, and that a certain harmony existed among them. They led a kind of brotherly life, naturally, and didn't scheme against one another. The more we are like them in this regard, the better it will be for us. It also seems as if the Japanese earned very little money and lived like simple workers. I have a reproduction (Bing published it) of 'A Single Blade of Grass.' What exemplary precision! You will see it some day." [B 18]

Vincent van Gogh to Émile Bernard, September/October 1888

UNDER THE SPELL OF JAPAN

In the spring of 1887, van Gogh organized an exhibit of Japanese prints in the Café du Tambourin (illus. p. 96). In fact, some of the prints, called *crépons* because of the thin paper used to make them, can even be recognized in the background of the portrait of Agostina Segatori (illus. p. 90). This illustrates the documentary aspect of van Gogh's work, which would become increasingly abstract over time and remain a characteristic feature of his art. Even though the exhibition did not attract a great deal of attention at the time, it nevertheless marked the beginning of Vincent's intensive study and incorporation of Japanese art in his own work. Incidentally, this also applied to works by his friend Bernard, whose "cloisonnistic" style was significantly inspired by the two-dimensional coloring and clear contours of traditional Japanese prints.

Typically, van Gogh's creative adoption of Japanese prints developed through copying a number of masterpieces that were his special favorites. He obtained them in large quantities from Bing, a shop that specialized in Japanese art. In the

fall of 1887, he painted three japonaiseries based on prints of woodcut masters, among them Utagawa Hiroshige's *Plum Garden at Kameido* (illus. above). Van Gogh's version follows the composition of the original down to the last detail (illus. opposite). Even the paper on which he carried out a screen transferral of the print has been preserved. However, his oil painting is not an exact replica, because it clearly distinguishes itself from Hiroshige's print through more forceful coloration. Another detail changes the picture's effect to a significant degree: the fruit blossoms in Hiroshige's print are clearly silhouetted in fine contours against the sky, but

△ **Utagawa Hiroshige** *Plum Garden at Kameido,* 1857, color woodcut, 14⅓ x 9⅔ in (36.3 x 24.6 cm), New York, Brooklyn Museum of Art

Page 98
Japonaiserie: Bridge in the Rain (after Hiroshige), 1887, oil on canvas, 28¾ x 21¼ in (73 x 54 cm), Amsterdam, Van Gogh Museum

Page 99
Japonaiserie: Oiran (after Kesaï Eisen), 1887, oil on canvas, 41½ x 23¾ in (105.5 x 60.5 cm), Amsterdam, Van Gogh Museum

Japonaiserie: Flowering Plum Tree (after Hiroshige), 1887,
oil on canvas, 21⅔ x 18 in (55 x 46 cm),
Amsterdam, Van Gogh Museum

Portrait of Père Tanguy, 1887, oil on canvas,
36¼ x 29½ in (92 x 75 cm), Paris, Musée Rodin

▷ *Italian Woman (Agostina Segatori?),* 1887, oil on canvas,
31¾ x 23⅔ in (81 x 60 cm), Paris, Musée d'Orsay

Still Life with French Novels and a Rose, 1887,
oil on canvas, 28¾ x 36¼ in (73 x 92 cm),
private collection

▷ *Self-Portrait with Straw Hat,* 1887,
oil on canvas on wood, 13⅓ x 10½ in (34 x 26.7 cm),
Detroit, Detroit Institute of Arts

in van Gogh's japonaiserie, they blend into the brightening dawn on the horizon to form a band of white, yellow, and rose-colored light. It is almost as if the landscape were festively illuminated, as if heaven and earth were radiantly united. Van Gogh apparently surpassed the original in order to visualize his idea of a utopian Japan, and at the same time the image becomes a good omen, since blossoms announce eternal renewal and the return of spring. The orange borders with black Japanese characters are also interesting, and van Gogh did not add them for purely decorative reasons. The frame lends a distracting tension to the work and appears to want to create the illusion of looking out a window, which is effectively offset by the stylized landscape. Yet the borders, and above all the kanji, bring out the pictorial quality of the painting and make reference to a deeper level

of meaning within the picture. *Japonaiserie: Flowering Plum Tree (after Hiroshige),* which to some extent anticipates the spring blossoms of Provence in van Gogh's later work, is also a programmatic painting and becomes a blueprint for Vincent's future artistic development.

Van Gogh's interest in Japanese prints extended beyond merely copying them. Their inspiration is apparent in several oil portraits completed during his last months in Paris. For example, he made a frontal portrait of his beloved "Père" Tanguy against a backdrop of Japanese prints, giving him the appearance of a resting Buddha, as has often been aptly noted (illus. p. 100). While this picture is technically similar to van Gogh's second self-portrait at the easel (illus. p. 75) and still suggests a spatial illusion, Vincent took a decisive step forward with his painting of an *Italian Woman* (illus. p. 101).

In that painting, likely another portrait of Agostina Segatori, he did nothing to conceal the two-dimensionality of the medium. The figure of the woman stands out only faintly from the bright yellow, almost monochromatic background. The "Japanese" simplicity of the picture is further emphasized by the two-sided faux frame, whose regularly spaced, brightly colored brush strokes lend it an ornamental character. These are carried over onto the picture itself, not only on the back of the chair, but also in the contrasting colors of the patterned skirt, the blouse, and even in the face of the woman in the portrait. Her face contains alternating red and green brush strokes suggestive of the tattooed countenance of someone from a primitive society. Van Gogh's effort to increase the expressiveness of the colors by simplifying the execution is clearly palpable. The colors are entirely disconnected from the subject and become an autonomous compositional element. Van Gogh's painting *Italian Woman* seems to have already anticipated fauvism.

YEARNING FOR THE SOUTH

For van Gogh, yellow was a symbol of the south, the color of sun and summertime. And the more concrete the idea of going to southern France became, the more yellow became the dominant color in Vincent's pictures. At first it appeared mainly in the form of the yellow straw hat that Vincent wore with his blue painter's smock, and in many self-portraits from the summer of 1887 it became a veritable emblem for his wanderlust (illus. p. 103). Thus, *Self-Portrait with Straw Hat* (illus. p. 9), painted on canvas with a sketchy lightness, gives insight into the liberation that van Gogh hoped another move would bring.

A first series of sunflower pictures also came about in the late summer (illus. opposite), anticipating the famous sunflower pictures he would paint in Arles in the following two years. Although the sunflowers in this earlier picture are cut and faded, van Gogh still gave them tremendous vitality.

He was apparently fascinated by the complexity of the surface structure of the flowers, which he reproduced with great care and very flexible brushstrokes. But what enchanted him most of all was their powerful orange-yellow petals, which van Gogh very effectively contrasted with blue, green, and violet, so that the flowers almost took on the appearance of lambent fireballs.

As he had previously done in Nuenen, van Gogh turned his attention that fall to a number of compositions with fruit and vegetables. Strongly contrasting colors are evident in these still lifes, as is the virtuosity with which he varied his brush technique, revealing the striking development that van Gogh had undergone in the previous two years. One picture deserves special recognition, and not only because he dedicated it to his brother Theo. In *Still Life with Grapes, Pears, and Lemons* (illus. opposite), he brought together his enthusiasm for Japan with his yearning for the south in yet another decisive work.

In its composition, this still life seems to reinterpret the very similar studies of potatoes van Gogh produced during his period in Nuenen by means of an entirely new color scheme. The dark, tone-in-tone Dutch color scheme has now become a brightly colored composition in yellow. Van Gogh demonstrates his ability as a colorist, highlighting the effect of the yellow with very delicate accents in red, violet, green, and blue; but also calming it down in spots with white. The color of the fruit carries over onto the yellow background and even the yellow frame, upon which stylized Japanese characters create an allusion to *crépons*. The frame thus becomes part of the composition, yet it also opens up the composition beyond its borders. The yellow appears to push its way out into the visual space, so much so that it looks as if it wants to usurp reality. For van Gogh, this was an idea that he wished would become reality. In mid-February of 1888, despite being very ill again, he packed his bags, boarded a train, and headed for Arles in Provence.

◁ *Still Life with Grapes, Pears, and Lemons*, 1887,
oil on canvas, 19 x 25½ in (48.5 x 65 cm),
Amsterdam, Van Gogh Museum

Two Cut Sunflowers, 1887,
oil on canvas, 17 x 24 in (43.2 x 61 cm),
New York, Metropolitan Museum of Art

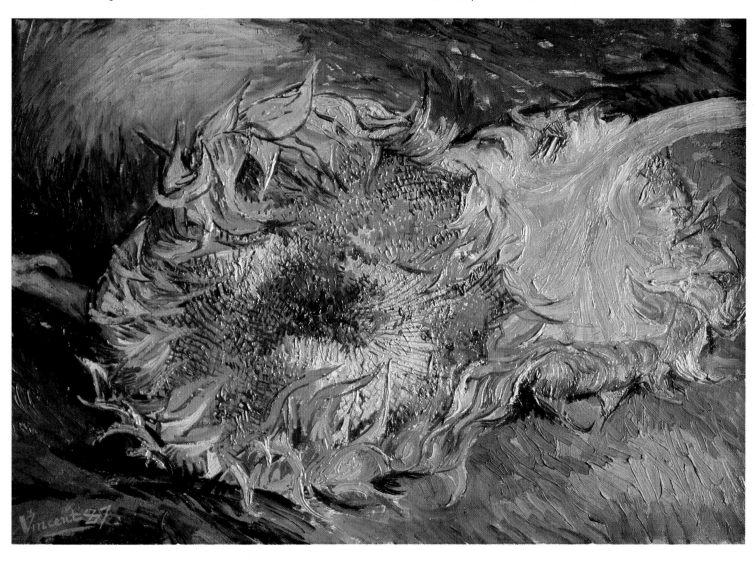

VAN GOGH AND THE ART TRADE

Legend has it that van Gogh's work—which today is bought and sold for some of the highest prices on record—generated little interest in the art market, and that he sold only one painting during his lifetime. Vincent's letters to Theo, however, reveal that in truth van Gogh had a very complicated and contradictory relationship with the business of art.

On February 8, 2003, this unsigned painting, which is presumed to have been painted by van Gogh, was sold in Tokyo for US $550,000.

There is no question that Vincent van Gogh was fully aware of the rules of art dealership, because three of his father's brothers were in the business. One of them, Uncle Cent, was even one of the partners of Goupil & Cie, a well-known art dealership with offices in several cities, where both Vincent and Theo learned the sales profession. Vincent, unlike his brother, finally terminated his career in art sales after seven years in the business. But since he kept up an intensive correspondence with Theo, who supported Vincent financially throughout the entire period of his artistic creativity, he always remained well informed about the current trends in the art market. Vincent tried to put his knowledge and contacts to use, and considering his financially dependent situation, he did so not only to help artists who were friends of his, such as Paul Gauguin, but also to further his own best interests. His efforts to convince Theo to establish himself as an independent art dealer were thus due at least in part to Vincent's desire to be able to better market his own work.

Although Vincent repeatedly expressed his contempt for the art dealing establishment, commercial considerations nonetheless had a direct influence on his artistic production at times—and not only at the outset of his career, when he was playing with the idea of earning a living by illustrating books. In Antwerp and Paris, he apparently produced a high volume of paintings and self-portraits for the purpose of advertising himself as a portraitist. The series of blooming fruit orchards in Arles, on the other hand, demonstrates that van Gogh produced variations of some attractive motifs because he believed in their market potential. As is well known, this dream was never fulfilled.

The Red Vineyard (illus. opposite), which was also completed in Arles, is often cited as the only painting that van Gogh sold in his lifetime. In fact, there is substantial evidence of additional sales, but those sales should be seen as exceptions to the rule, as should the pittance Vincent received from his Uncle Cor at the beginning of his career for several cityscapes of The Hague and the art supplies he was given as compensation for designing wall paintings during his time in Nuenen. What seems more significant is that by selective exchange of pictures, Vincent built up a collection that was intended to serve as the basis for Theo's planned art dealership, and as such undoubtedly had a certain market value. Even if the romantic idea of an idealistic genius painter who devoted himself entirely to his art must be relativized a bit, one thing can certainly stay on record: during his lifetime, van Gogh was far from being able to feed himself by the work of his own hands. For someone like him, who glorified peasant life as ideal, this was not only an enormous burden, but surely also a painful flaw.

In light of the cool reception that Vincent received from collectors and art dealers during his lifetime despite his best efforts, the posthumous value of his works seems all the more spectacular. *The Red Vineyard* sold for only 400 francs in 1890, a sum that was at the lower end of the art market in those days. Yet shortly after the turn of the century, van Gogh would be considered the most expensive modern artist of all. In the period before World War I, particularly in Germany, France, and the Netherlands, van Gogh's reputation as a high-status painter was launched to a great extent through the efforts of Theo's widow, Johanna van Gogh, as well as

The Red Vineyard, 1888, oil on canvas,
29½ x 36⅔ in (75 x 93 cm), Moscow, Pushkin Museum

several specialists; Vincent's life story was increasingly over-shadowed by the cultivation of the myth. Van Gogh's paintings were not only promoted as coveted collector's items; they also became a sought-after commodity that promised a quick maximum return, because Johanna van Gogh, in her capacity as executor of the estate, kept them in short supply. But that development also led to a large number of forgeries that quickly came onto the market, some of which were so convincing that Jacob Baart de la Faille entered them into the catalogue of van Gogh's works.

Since that time, van Gogh's paintings and drawings have never forfeited their leading position within the art market—on the contrary. In the 1980s, when large banks, corporations, and the ultrarich discovered modern art as a crisis-proof investment and signaled a bull market in the auction sector the likes of which had never existed before, van Gogh's *Irises* (illus. pp. 180–181) established a record that made headlines

worldwide: an Australian industrialist purchased the oil painting, which originated in Saint-Rémy, at a Sotheby's auction in November 1987 for a record sum of over $50 million. Less than three years later, in May 1990, *Irises* lost its standing as the most expensive van Gogh painting ever sold at auction when his *Portrait of Doctor Paul Gachet* (illus. p. 203) was purchased at Christie's by a wealthy Japanese art aficionado for $82.5 million. Today, prices seem to have stabilized, but even van Gogh's less renowned oil paintings have long since fetched amounts in the millions.

The enormous value of van Gogh's works has frequently made them targets of art theft. In February 2008, a raid on the E. G. Bührle Collection in Zurich, in which armed robbers absconded with four valuable paintings, including van Gogh's *Blossoming Chestnut Branches*, made headlines. Fortunately, the painting was recovered just a few days after the robbery took place.

IV. HIGHPOINT: ARLES (1888–1889)

HIGHPOINT: ARLES

SNOWY ARRIVAL

There may have been many motivations for van Gogh to head for Provence, but the strong desire "to see another kind of light" was the decisive one. "I thought that observing nature under a brighter sky would lead to a better understanding of the way the Japanese perceive and draw. I wanted to finally see this more intense sunlight, because a person who does not know it feels as if he cannot understand Delacroix's pictures from a technical standpoint, and because one feels as if the primary colors in the north are veiled by fog." [605]

In Provence, which was Monticelli's birthplace, van Gogh wanted to explore the secrets of Delacroix and the Japanese masters. It seems remarkable that unlike Monet, who also worked regularly in southern France, Vincent chose to settle in Arles, rather than on the Côte d'Azur. Arles, a city on the Rhône River, is not exactly counted among the most picturesque spots in Provence. It lies between the swampy areas of the Camargue and the agricultural La Crau lowlands, a good fifteen miles inland from the Mediterranean Sea, and despite its impressive Roman buildings and medieval churches, it is not so much a seaside idyll as an average, southern provincial city going about its daily activities. The Industrial Age had left its traces on the town in the form of the railroad and factories, and since a regiment of the Zouaves was quartered in Arles, a tavern and red-light district had also developed. There were hardly any tourists in Arles in those days.

It was apparently precisely that mixture of agricultural environment and vibrant provinciality that inspired van Gogh and incited him to work at a pace that bordered on the maniacal. In the fifteen months he resided in Arles, he created a body of work that rightly counts as the highpoint of his career, and is without parallel in the history of art. It

comprises about two hundred paintings, more than a hundred drawings and watercolors, and over two hundred letters.

Van Gogh's arrival in Arles was anything but auspicious. When his train from Paris arrived at the railway station in Arles on February 20, he was in for a big surprise. Instead of the early spring weather he had been expecting, he was greeted by snow. Nonetheless, although it remained cold for several more weeks, as soon as he had gotten settled into a modest hotel, Vincent went straight to work. Just a few days later he wrote to Theo about the first oil studies: "an old Arlesienne, a snowy landscape, a bit of sidewalk with a butcher's shop." [464]

Since the frost made working in the outdoors impossible, van Gogh turned to painting still lifes again. A small oil painting from those days, a flowering almond branch in a glass, clearly shows that Vincent had meanwhile become a master colorist (illus. opposite). Although the "Japanese" motif is realized with the greatest simplicity, the picture conveys an intensely colorful impression that expresses the joyful anticipation of spring. The strong red line drawn horizontally through the neutral gray background is of special interest. The line can be explained as a wall decoration, yet it also represents a completely autonomous—and abstract—element of the composition that not only provides structure within the pictorial space, but, above all, contrasts with the cool colors in the lower half of the picture. Van Gogh's signature of the painting in the same warm red as the line adds an additional demonstrative note to the boldness of this apparently modern element.

SPRING IN PROVENCE

Blossoming Almond Branch in a Glass was basically the prologue to a series of fourteen oil paintings that van Gogh produced in March and April 1888 in celebration of fruit blossoms in Provence. It is entirely possible that the prospect of such a display of nature was decisive in van Gogh's decision to travel to Arles in the spring. His copy of Hiroshige's print supports the supposition that van Gogh may already have had the idea for such a cycle while he was in Paris, and the

▷ *Blossoming Almond Branch in a Glass*, 1888, oil on canvas, 9½ x 7½ in (24 x 19 cm), Amsterdam, Van Gogh Museum

Pages 108–109
Harvest in Provence (detail), 1888, oil on canvas,
19¾ x 23⅔ in (50 x 60 cm), Jerusalem, Israel Museum

Japanese woodcut may not necessarily have served as his the sole source of inspiration. At that time, van Gogh must have also been familiar, for example, with Daubigny's flowering gardens.

In light of his spiritual sensibility, it is plausible that van Gogh also attributed symbolic meaning to the fruit blossom motif, bringing to mind that infinite and divine nature that awakens to new life each spring. Undoubtedly, van Gogh hoped for a new beginning in Arles, or at the very least, a renewal of his creative energy. However, there was another more pragmatic motive for the series. Van Gogh, who was very clearly aware of how attractive this theme was, was firmly resolved to succeed in the art market henceforth, and to achieve recognition in his homeland. This also meant that he wanted to convince Tersteeg of his abilities. Theo was planning to distribute the impressionists' work outside France with the help of Vincent's former boss, of all people. For this reason, contact between them had again intensified. So it was that van Gogh dedicated his picture of a blossoming peach tree to his teacher, Mauve, who had recently died, and gave it to Mauve's widow as a gift. This gesture was not only motivated by his grief, but also by tactical considerations. After all, Vincent's cousin had been among the established greats in the Dutch art trade until the time of his death.

It may seem completely paradoxical that the painting *Pink Peach Tree in Blossom*, which also bears the title *Reminiscence of Mauve* (illus. p. 115), shows no traces at all of the style of the Hague school. Vincent made no apparent acknowledgement of the Hague school, neither in the style nor in the palette. "You will understand," he stated in a letter to Wil, "that the palette of a Mauve, for example, can never properly express the nature of the south. Mauve belongs to the north; he is and remains a master of the gray. But today's palette is colorful through and through: sky blue, orange, pink, vermillion, brilliant yellow, bright green, clear wine red, violet. But if one intensifies all the colors, one again comes to a point of harmony and calm." [W 3]

Vincent certainly realized that his painting style would meet with opposition. "My brush strokes do not belong to any particular school of technique," he reported to Bernard concerning his work on the fruit orchard series. "I slap irregular brush strokes on the canvas and leave them that way. Thick blotches of color, bare spots on the canvas, a completely unfinished corner here and there, overpainting, rawness—in short, I fear the result is rather disturbing and annoying, and will not please people with preconceived ideas about technique." [B 3] Apparently, Vincent was so

The White Orchard, 1888,
oil on canvas, 23⅔ x 31¾ in (60 x 81 cm),
Amsterdam, Van Gogh Museum

Pink Peach Tree in Blossom (Reminiscence of Mauve), 1888,
oil on canvas, 28¾ x 23½ in (73 x 59.5 cm),
Otterlo, Kröller-Müller Museum

◁ *Blossoming Pear Tree,* 1888,
oil on canvas, 28¾ x 18 in (73 x 46 cm),
Amsterdam, Van Gogh Museum

The Langlois Bridge at Arles, 1888, oil on canvas,
19½ x 25¼ in (49.5 x 64 cm), Cologne, Wallraf-Richartz Museum

▷ *The Langlois Bridge at Arles*, 1888
watercolor on paper, private collection

sure of the quality of his "disturbing" and "annoying"works that he dared to send them to Holland anyway, even though his efforts met with no response.

The letter addressed to his friend and fellow artist indicates that van Gogh's painting tempo not only sped up further, but as he experienced nature coming into bloom, his painting style became even more spontaneous and intuitive. Spring in Provence stimulated Vincent's creative impulse. "I always work directly on site and try to capture the essence of the scene in the sketch—the surfaces, which are defined by contours that may or may not be present, but are always felt. Then I fill these in with simplified colors in such a way that everything that is terrain gets painted in the same shade of violet, everything that is sky is in the same shade of blue, and everything that is green becomes either blue-green or yellow-green, whereby I exaggerate the yellow or blue tones, as the case may be. In short, dear friend, at least this is no trompe l'oeil painting." [B 3]

If impressionism had taught van Gogh to use colors less self-consciously, then Japanese prints prompted him to increase the intensity of his colors, to consciously exaggerate them. From this point on, he "filled in" the "felt" contours with "simplified colors." In the process, however, he always started with tangible reality. For van Gogh, who sought the expression of the inner life—the very soul—through art, hypernaturalistic trompe l'oeil painting was a cold portrayal, like photography. For his passion to be ignited, however, he needed genuine subject matter, a model. He was not able to accomplish this in the Parisian metropolis. The spark was lit only now, in the south of France, and his painting displayed a power that he had envisioned for a long time.

Also interesting about the fruit orchard series is that van Gogh intended to arrange the paintings as three-part *décorations* or triptychs, consisting of an upright format in the center and two landscape formats to the sides. He was only able to realize this in stages, because the mistral—a treacherous, cold, northwest wind—made it difficult to work outdoors while the fruit trees were in bloom. However, the project illuminates not only how important the religious aspect was to Vincent (the triptych form references medieval winged altars), but also how fundamental the decorative role of art was to him. Since his works are usually seen in museums today, it is easy to forget that they were intended to be displayed in living spaces and were meant to enrich people's daily lives. In the same way, van Gogh surrounded himself in his own rooms with pictures that inspired and comforted him.

THE BRIDGE AT ARLES

His first months in Arles were among the most productive in van Gogh's ten-year-long period of creativity. He told his brother that he was in a "constant state of feverish work." Unlike when he was in Paris, Vincent seemed to adjust to the unfamiliar surroundings rather quickly, possibly in part because he saw similarities between Provence in the south of France and his homeland, especially in the ditches and canals that traversed the La Crau lowlands. "Many of the motifs here

Drawing in van Gogh's letter of several pages to Émile Bernard, March 18, 1888, private collection

contrast between the bright blue of the sky, which is mirrored in the water, and the powerful, "exaggerated" yellow of the embankments on both sides of the canal. These blue and yellow sections come together in the area of the bridge, whereby the structure becomes a place of transition in multiple respects. Not only does it bridge a body of water, but through color, it also unites the natural elements—namely air, earth, and water—at the very center of the painting.

The coloring of the picture does not correspond to the objective reality van Gogh encountered and is particularly noticeable in terms of one detail: the blue inner wall of the bridge clearly does not accord with the actual color scheme, but is instead the result of unambiguous conceptual considerations. Likewise, the pale, flat green that can be seen between the walls gives only a vague suggestion of what lies hidden behind the structure. So the bridge seems to be a kind of gateway, as it were, into a mysterious realm that is unportrayable. The secretive aura is amplified by the carriage and the black figure on the bridge, which stand in peculiar contradiction to the vital color scheme of the picture. Here, too, this world and the next seem to come together, generating a tension that infuses van Gogh's entire work.

SUMMER IN THE SOUTH

With the beginning of the warm season, van Gogh was enticed more and more often to work in the area surrounding Arles. This was also partly due to a lack of available models in Arles. The main destinations of these sojourns were the intensively farmed acreage and fields of the La Crau lowlands and Montmajour, a rock formation with the ruin of a large abbey that offered a fantastic view onto the flat agricultural lands. Because his financial situation became precarious when Theo had a fight with his boss, Vincent again turned increasingly to drawing. This not only saved money, but also meant significantly less time and effort spent working outside the studio. Thus, between May and July, van Gogh produced a series of reed pen drawings that captured the ruins of the Benedictine abbey and wide panoramas inspired by seventeenth-century Dutch landscape painting. Van Gogh placed great importance on drawing not only at the start of his artistic career, but continued to do so at the height of his creativity. The works from his time in Arles were definitely not conceived merely as drafts or sketches that he attached to letters in order to convey an impression to Theo and his friends of the content of his paintings. Van Gogh often regarded them as independent, equally valuable works, and not infrequently even used paintings as models for his drawings. In particular, the rich body of drawings from the last two years of his life is invaluable.

have the same character as in Holland," he wrote to Theo in May. "The difference lies in the colors. Wherever things are bathed in sunlight, there is sulphur yellow." [488] A subject that seems to illustrate this comment especially well is the Pont de Langlois (Langlois Bridge), a railroad bridge south of the Arles city limits that Vincent captured in numerous paintings, watercolors, and drawings that spring. Presumably, he was simply in error when he called it Pont de l'Anglais (English Bridge).

The Langlois Bridge at Arles (illus. p. 116), an oil painting that he completed in May 1888, creates a special tension as it unites the "Dutch" aspect of the Provençal landscape with van Gogh's vision of the "Japanese south." On the one hand, the pictorial motif establishes a strong connection to Vincent's homeland, similar to the windmills of the Butte de Montmartre. Thus, even the figure with an umbrella on the bridge, apparently a woman from Arles in local garb, suggests that she could just as well be a Calvinist woman dressed in black. On the other hand, van Gogh's artistic execution of the scene clearly references the inspiration he derived from Japanese prints. The clearly structured composition and two-dimensional coloration are manifestly based on the prototype of the Far Eastern woodcut masters. The design of the bridge is reminiscent of filigreed Japanese wooden architecture.

The bridge, which is the focal point of the picture, evidently represents more than just a picturesque motif: Van Gogh painted it as an emblem of transcendence. The color scheme thereby takes on decisive meaning, because the picture's impact is derived to a great extent from the stark

The Painter on His Way to Work, 1888,
oil on canvas, 19 x 17⅓ in (48 x 44 cm),
destroyed by fire in World War II

During the spring and summer, Vincent hiked through the area around
Arles, almost daily at times, in order to draw or paint. He is easily
identified by the red beard and straw hat, portraying himself in this
picture "laden with a box of paints, brushes, and canvas, on the road
to Tarascon under a blistering sun." [524]

On May 30, 1888, van Gogh set out by train to spend four days in Saintes-Maries-de-la-Mer, a small pilgrimage town just twenty-five miles away on the coast. While there he devoted himself mainly to drawing, but also produced watercolors and two seascapes in oil (illus. below and right). Significantly, Vincent's interest was not piqued by the town's pilgrimage sites, but rather by the colorful sailboats and fishermen's cottages. The sweeping, spontaneous, and energetic lines he used to reproduce the maritime motifs on paper give an idea of how much he enjoyed the Mediterranean setting, notwithstanding that they reminded him of Scheveningen in Holland. Even though this would be van Gogh's only excursion to the Mediterranean Sea, traces of the experience can be found in his work. "Now that I have seen the sea here," he wrote euphorically to Theo, "I can really feel how important it is to remain in the south and to perceive the need to exaggerate the colors even more, because it is not much further to Africa." [500]

Vincent's longing to see Africa was surely connected to his admiration for Delacroix, whose use of color was deeply influenced by a trip to Africa. This comment also shows how much van Gogh understood his own work in the context of a more far-reaching endeavor. Since his time in Paris, he had seen himself as part of the avant-garde, which, far away from the civilization found in big cities, wanted to promote the regeneration of art through the creative adoption of pure, original forms of expression. He had this goal in common with Gauguin, Bernard, and several other like-minded people. Like his artist friends, who launched cloissonism during the summer in secluded Pont-Aven in Brittany, Vincent found his inspiration to a great extent in folk art and Japanese prints.

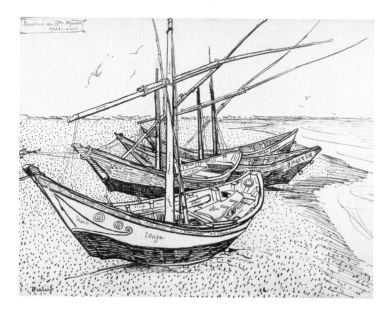

Fishing Boats on the Beach at Saintes-Maries, 1888, reed pen with ink on paper, 15½ x 21 in (39.5 x 53.6 cm), private collection

▷ *Fishing Boats on the Beach at Saintes-Maries*, 1888, oil on canvas, 25½ x 32 in (65 x 81.5 cm), Amsterdam, Van Gogh Museum

Street in Saintes-Maries, 1888, oil on canvas,
15 x 18 in (38.3 x 46.1 cm), private collection

▷ *Haystacks in Provence*, 1888, oil on canvas,
29 x 36⅔ in (73.5 x 93 cm), Otterlo, Kröller-Müller Museum

The oil paintings, which he created from drawings after his return to Arles from Saintes-Maries, show this with absolute clarity. The richly contrasting, powerful colors and the flat composition of the pictures attest to his desire for a radically simplified formal language that stood in irreconcilable opposition to the bourgeois perception of what constituted art, and was perceived to be decadent.

HARVEST TIME

In June, van Gogh turned his attention to a subject that he had already worked on in his homeland. He wanted to capture the harvest in his pictures. In contrast to the works he produced in Holland, however, his focus was less on farm labor itself. Instead, the work of reaping, bundling, and transporting grain was subordinated to portrayal of the landscape, within which the peasants are only seen as small figures, integral parts of nature, which is reformed through agriculture, as in Japanese prints.

The powerful radiance of the yellow in these works, which Vincent elevated to a symbol of summertime and the south, is a major reason why the harvest paintings have made such a significant contribution to the popular myth of van Gogh. It undoubtedly also explains why the paintings are considerably better known than the drawings, which are superb. In the colorful intensity of the series, van Gogh not only displayed the richness and vitality of creation, he also focused attention on the physical aspect of painting. "A week of intense, hard work in the fields under the hot sun is behind me," [501] he mentioned in a letter to Theo in June. Looking at the paintings, one can vividly imagine Vincent setting up his easel in the torrid heat of the cornfields and working to the point of physical exhaustion (illus. below and following). That he would consciously expose himself to suffering and intentionally wear himself to the bone reflects his tendency toward self-mortification. "During harvest time, my work was no easier than that of the peasants, who were bringing in the harvest with their own hands," he wrote to Theo several weeks later. "But I am in no way complaining, for these are precisely the times when I feel nearly as happy in the artistic life, even if it isn't real life, as I could be in an ideal, real life." [507] Vincent's identification with peasant life effectively reached its high point in his pictures of harvest time in Provence. Painting became his form of field work.

Among the oil paintings he created during the summer months was one that van Gogh especially prized, a panorama of the La Crau lowlands with Montmajour and the Alpille Mountains in the background (illus. p. 127). He had already drawn this scene, which, according to his own statements, was inspired by the landscape panoramas of the Dutch baroque painter Philips Koninck (illus. foldout). Because of its rich detail, as well as the enhanced viewpoint of the observer, the picture Vincent himself called simply *"Harvest"* is rather atypical of his oil paintings from that summer. According to his own evaluation, however, the fact that it "beat" all his other pictures "hands down" lay mainly in the "strength of the colors," [497] which he saw as trendsetting.

Actually, this painting is an especially successful example of van Gogh's stated intention to attain harmony by means of color intensification. Although yellow and blue—the colors of summer in Provence—are dominant, the picture nevertheless unifies all the primary and secondary colors into a lively

Wheat Field with Sheaves, 1888, oil on canvas,
20¾ x 25¼ in (53 x 64 cm), Honolulu, Honolulu Academy of Arts

▷ *Arles : View from the Wheat Fields*, 1888,
oil on canvas, 28¾ x 21¼ in (73 x 54 cm), Paris, Musée Rodin

interplay of contrasting surfaces. The intense constellations that arise in the details dissolve almost musically in the composition as a whole. The placement of the cart in the center of the painting draws the observer's attention to it and shows just how carefully the picture was put together. On the one hand, the cart's privileged position brings the object to the forefront as a carrier of meaning. The cart could be interpreted as a symbol of peasants' work, or equally convincingly as an allegory for the integration of the harvest into the eternal cycle of nature. At the same time, the wagon adds a strong color accent: as with the blue, shady side of the houses, the blue cart also creates an association between itself and the surrounding cornfields, as well as the blue of the sky and mountains.

As in other harvest pictures from 1888, the peasants in this painting can only be made out as tiny figures. However, farm labor itself has an even greater presence within the depicted landscape, less as an encroachment upon nature and more as part of a divine order. The picture thus suggests that van Gogh's fascination with Jean-François Millet, which had temporarily receded into the background in Antwerp and Paris, was reawakened by his impressions of Provence in southern France. During harvest time in Arles, van Gogh found many motifs that Millet had already worked with, such as sheaves of wheat and piles of straw. Most importantly, he rediscovered a figure that would reappear in van Gogh's work, one which had held great meaning for him at the beginning of his artistic career: the sower.

A SOWER IN COLOR

It was in late June, 1888, that Vincent reported to his brother about a sketch of a sower. "On a plowed field, a large field of violet earth in clumps that ascends toward the horizon—a sower in blue and white. A low field of ripe corn on the horizon. A yellow sky with a golden sun above the entire scene. You'll note from this simple description of the tonal values that color plays an important role in the composition." He continued, "I have been wanting to do a sower for ages, but the desires I've had for a long time do not always come true. I am almost fearful about it. Still, what remains to be done in the style of Millet and Lhermitte is the sower—in color and in large format." [501]

Vincent's trepidation is understandable, given that what he had in mind was nothing less than to bring together the work of two of his esteemed role models (quasi father figures), to unite the spiritual power and simplicity of Millet

with Delacroix's use of color, which he understood as a symbolic language. In the following days and weeks, he was obsessed with this project. "I worked on the 'Sower' both yesterday and today, and have totally altered him," he wrote to Theo again just a few days later. "The sky is yellow and green, the ground violet and orange. A picture could surely be made from this superb motif, and I hope that it will be painted some day, whether by me or someone else." [503] In fact, Vincent did make a painting based on the sketches, and *The Sower* is among the most exceptional works of his Arles period (illus. pp. 128–129). Unlike any of his previous works, it deals with the symbolist concepts of his artist friends from Pont-Aven, although it certainly does not borrow from them wholesale.

Although the sketches were done outdoors, the painstaking pointillistic brushstroke and dotted techniques lead to the assumption that the painting was mainly completed in the studio. The distracting fact that it depicts an activity that seems entirely paradoxical in high summer clearly reveals that while the picture was inspired by the traditional agricultural calendar, it did not result from direct observation of nature, but rather from the commitment to an overriding idea. The same is true of the enormous setting sun in the middle of the horizon and the figure of the sower, of course, which is a direct adaptation of Millet's peasant imagery. Van Gogh apparently intended to once again portray the cycle of ripening, dying off, and regeneration in his *Sower*. Indeed, the idea first takes definitive shape through the symbolic energy of the colors: the warm gold of the sun, which extends over the entire sky in orange-yellow rays and spills over onto the field of ripe corn; the plowed field, in contrast, rendered in blue and violet yet literally dotted with orange-colored flecks, so that it seems as if the sower were immediately carrying over the life-giving power of the sun onto the earth. Van Gogh himself regarded the picture as "a failure." [522]

PORTRAITIST

However much the people and the landscape of the Midi-Pyrénées inspired van Gogh, he still had to deal with an old, familiar problem in Arles: the lack of models. He loved Alphonse Daudet's lively descriptions of the Provençal mentality and Zola's powerful character studies, and he admired Honoré Daumier's caricatures and Frans Hals' vivacious portraits. So this lack of models must have been deeply disappointing to him, particularly since making works of art that were accessible to the masses had been an essential driving force of his creativity from the very beginning. Vincent's was a social and, in the best sense of the word, a humanistic art that was intended to keep people grounded and to bestow confidence, while giving expression to the value of the simple life. Vincent's relief must have been great when, in June, he was able to relate to Theo that he had found a model. "A Zouave, a small fellow

◁ *Harvest in Provence*, 1888, oil on canvas, 19¾ x 23⅔ in (50 x 60 cm), Jerusalem, Israel Museum

Harvest at La Crau, with Montmajour in the Background, 1888, oil on canvas, 28¾ x 36¼ in (73 x 92 cm), Amsterdam, Van Gogh Museum

with a bull neck and the eyes of a tiger. I started one portrait, and then began all over again with a second one." [501]

The second of these portraits of the North African soldier, especially, is highly original (illus. p. 130). It shows a simple man—in front of a white wall and facing toward the viewer, in an extremely colorful uniform—sitting on a low stool with his legs wide apart. The model's animal sensuality, as intimated in Vincent's letter, has been forcefully developed in the portrait. The orange-colored harem pants, in particular, are nearly as wide as the picture itself and virtually burst into view. In their plasticity, only vaguely fashioned by means of rough brush strokes, they form an enormous, translucent triangle that points toward the center of the Zouave's body. His vitality is further emphasized by the position of his left hand, which rests on his upper inner thigh. The man looks directly at the observer, decidedly self-confident. The whole effect is one of startling naturalness.

Also apparent is that, as in the portrait of the *Italian Woman* (illus. p. 101), van Gogh barely develops a sense of depth; the white background remains perfectly flat. Like the man's pants, the uniform jacket with its ornamental flourishes looks almost two-dimensional. However, the artist's refusal to play by the rules of perspective is most clearly seen in the tiled floor, over which the Zouave's feet seem to almost float. This gives the man a kind of dance-like airiness, such as that found in Japanese figurative representations. But van Gogh was unhappy with both portraits; he actually described them as ugly. "Still," he wrote to his brother, "figures interest me much more than landscapes." [502]

Vincent was later able to obtain several natives of the region as models, which suggests that he had, by then, met with a certain acceptance in Arles. So it was that he painted *La Mousmé* (illus. p. 133), inspired by Pierre Loti's novel, *Madame Chrysanthème*: "a young Japanese girl—in this case, a Provençal girl—between twelve and fourteen years old." [514] Suffering from persistent stomach trouble, it took van Gogh a week to complete the portrait, which he worked on with exceptional diligence and the finest color accentuation, particularly in the area of the face. He was wonderfully successful in capturing the shyness, youthful freshness, and feminine grace of the young girl and, at the same time, in imparting a sense of the woman she would become. Her more mature physique already seems to emerge in the curves of the armchair, which carry over into the curves of the ornamental skirt, conspicuously flat and reminiscent of the styling in *The Seated Zouave*.

When he first arrived in Arles, van Gogh socialized only with the young Danish painter Christian Mourier-Petersen.

The Sower, 1888,
oil on canvas, 25¼ x 31⅔ in (64.2 x 80.3 cm),
Otterlo, Kröller-Müller Museum

The Seated Zouave, 1888,
oil on canvas, 31¾ x 25⅔ in (81 x 65 cm),
private collection

Portrait of Milliet, Second Lieutenant of the Zouaves, also known as *The Lover: Paul-Eugène Milliet*, 1888, oil on canvas, 23¾ x 19½ in (60.3 x 49.5 cm), Otterlo, Kröller-Müller Museum

La Mousmé, Sitting, 1888,
pen and ink on paper, 12¾ x 9⅔ in (32.5 x 24.5 cm),
Moscow, Pushkin Museum

But during the course of the summer, Vincent made new contacts. One of his acquaintances was Second Lieutenant Paul-Eugène Milliet, who had helped him establish contact with the Zouave model, and who went on walking tours and forays through the city's establishments with him. Vincent also did his portrait (illus. p. 131), depicting him as a lover, since van Gogh was impressed with the effect the officer had on women (the painting is also known as *The Lover, Paul-Eugène Milliet*).

At the beginning of August, Vincent told his brother about another model. "This one is a postman in a blue uniform with gold trim, and a coarse, bearded face, quite the Socrates. A rabid French Republican like Father. A man who is considerably more interesting than many other folk." [516] This person, who first sat as a model for two portraits (illus. p. 134), was named Joseph Roulin. Not only would van Gogh paint Roulin and his entire family many times in the coming months, but Roulin would also come to be a trusted friend who stood faithfully by Vincent's side when catastrophe hit him at the end of the year.

Shortly after meeting Roulin, van Gogh was able to make a portrait of a peasant again for the first time since his Nuenen

period (illus. p. 135). "Soon," he happily announced to his brother, "you will meet the honorable Patience Escalier, a real 'man with a hoe.' He is an old ox herder from the Camargue and now works as a gardener at a country house in La Crau." Vincent had once again arrived at his favorite theme, as his allusion to Millet's painting *Man with a Hoe* clearly revealed. "I have noticed," he wrote in addition, "that everything I learned in Paris is vanishing, and I have returned to the ideas that I had earlier in the country, before I ever met the impressionists." [520]

The colorfulness of the *Portrait of Patience Escalier*, however, has nothing in common with the dark tone-on-tone palette of *The Potato Eaters* (illus. pp. 52–53). "I imagined the frightening man I was about to create, at the height of the midday heat during the sweltering harvest time. That's the reason for the blazing orange, akin to a red-hot forge, and for the tones of luminous old gold in the shadows." Van Gogh had increasingly distanced himself from the impressionist approach, and it was entirely conscious. "Instead of simply reproducing what is before my eyes, I avail myself of color more arbitrarily, in order to express myself more powerfully." [520] In Arles, Vincent's unmistakable expressionist art began to fully unfold. And as a portraitist, he now had the goal of his artistic vision right before his eyes. "I would like to say something consoling with a picture, as music does. I would like to paint men and women with a certain eternal quality, like the halo used to symbolize, something we try to express through illumination, through vibrating and pulsating colors." [531]

That summer, through his American artist friend, Dodge MacKnight, who lived in the neighboring village of Fontvieille, van Gogh met the young Belgian writer and painter Eugène Boch. Vincent felt a kind of spiritual affinity with Boch, the sensitive, artistically inclined son of an industrialist from Borinage, even if he described Boch's painting to Theo as "docile impressionism." [528] Like van Gogh, Boch was also concerned with social issues. Boch was making plans to return to his homeland to paint miners, most likely inspired by the stories of his friend, who was two years his elder. In 1890, Boch's sister Anna, also a painter and closely associated with the Brussels group *Les Vingts*, purchased van Gogh's painting *The Red Vineyard* (illus. p. 107). It is often cited as the only work of his that was sold during his lifetime (see p. 106 for further discussion of this).

In the portrait that van Gogh painted of Eugène Boch (illus. p. 137), the halo seems to take physical form. Vincent told his brother about his concept for the portrait in advance.

La Mousmé, 1888, oil on canvas,
29 x 23½ in (74 x 60 cm),
Washington D.C., National Gallery of Art

Portrait of the Postman Joseph Roulin, 1888, oil on canvas,
32 x 25¾ in (81.3 x 65.4 cm), Boston, Museum of Fine Arts, gift of Robert Treat Paine II

Portrait of Patience Escalier, 1888, oil on canvas,
27¼ x 22 in (69.2 x 56 cm), private collection

Starry Night Over the Rhone, 1888, oil on canvas, 28½ x 36¼ in (72.5 x 92 cm), Paris, Musée d'Orsay

▷ *Portrait of Eugène Boch,* 1888, oil on canvas, 23⅔ x 17¾ in (60 x 45 cm), Paris, Musée d'Orsay

"I would like to do the portrait of a friend, an artist, who dreams of great things and labors, even as the nightingale sings, because it is in his nature. This man will be blond. I would like to infuse the picture with the admiration and love I feel for him." In order to give expression to his feelings, Vincent wanted not only to "exaggerate" the blondness of the hair, but to also paint "infinity" for the background, "rather than the expressionless wall of the dingy room . . . . A plain background of the most luxurious and vivid blue I can muster, and by means of this simple configuration of the luminous blond head against the lush blue background, it will take on something mystical." [520] In the portrait, the intense blue background was conceived as a starry firmament, reflected in the form of a slender, orange-colored band of light at the back of the subject's head, as if the poet were surrounded by a halo and illuminated by eternity.

NIGHT PAINTINGS

The portrait of his friend alludes to an intention Vincent had voiced to Theo in the springtime. "I must have a starry night with cypresses," he wrote euphorically. "The nights are so beautiful here." [474] Van Gogh did not tackle the cypress image until the following year in Saint-Rémy (illus. pp. 186–187), but he acted on the plan to devote himself to nighttime plein air painting in Arles by means of two paintings late in the summer of 1888. Whether he thereby established himself as a pioneer in the history of art, as has sometimes been claimed, is open to question. However, painting in the dark obviously entails immense difficulties. The anecdote that he attached candles to the brim of his straw hat in order to be able to work at night is one of many stories about van Gogh that are widely circulated though they have little basis in fact.

Louis Anquetin *Street Scene, at Five in the Afternoon*, 1887,
oil and paper on canvas, 27¼ x 21¾ in (69.2 x 55.5 cm),
Hartford, CT, Wadsworth Atheneum Museum of Art

According to van Gogh's own account, one of the night pictures was painted beneath a gas lantern. It shows a clear, starry sky over the Rhone River, in which the lights of the city are reflected toward the observer in long, vertical lines (illus. p. 136). Blue and yellow contrasts also dominate this painting, but Vincent's description reveals his finely nuanced treatment. "The sky is blue-green, the water royal blue, and the ground mauve. The city is blue and violet, the gaslights are yellow; the reflections are golden red and extend all the way to bronze-green. In the blue-green firmament, Ursa Major, whose restrained pallor contrasts with the gaudy gold of the gaslights, sparkles in green and rose." [543] Once again, the boundaries between the heavenly and earthly spheres seem to dissolve. A couple wandering in the foreground, as so often happens with van Gogh, highlights the romantic feeling of the scene.

Because he chose a motif in the center of the city of Arles, the second night picture, *Café Terrace on the Place du Forum, Arles, at Night* (illus. opposite), has earned a special place in van Gogh's oeuvre from the Provençal period. Apparently, Louis Anquetin's painting *Street Scene, at Five in the Afternoon* (illus. above), served as inspiration—a Parisian, big-city impression,

which was shown at the Petit Boulevard exhibition van Gogh had organized the year before. Of course, Vincent's picture does nothing to mask the provinciality of the place. In contrast to the hectic hustle and bustle of the boulevard, it shows a quiet, narrow street in which the terrace of the eatery, lit up with yellow-orange light from gas lanterns, serves as the only center of attraction for the limited number of figures portrayed. So much so, that it is as if the night swarmers were magically attracted to the light like proverbial moths to a flame. As in van Gogh's view of the river, the collision of blue and yellow dominates the color impact of the picture. Upon closer inspection, though, an exceedingly rich palette becomes apparent. Vincent called his own work "a night scene without black." [W 7]

The painting certainly owes some of its attraction to the luminosity of the nighttime café, but its appeal is primarily due to the composition, which is characterized by lines that give depth to the pictorial space, whereby van Gogh bends the rules of central perspective representation just as liberally as he habitually "exaggerates" colors. The picture is also an excellent example of the color and form analogies that are repeatedly found in van Gogh's most important works. The dark blue sky, for example, which tapers to a point in the center of the picture, contains disc-like shining stars, and finds its analogue in the orange-colored terrace and the white tabletops. This is a perceived analogy, which further illustrates the extent to which van Gogh transformed existing situations into subjective reality in his works.

The murky carriage approaching from the depths of the street canyon looks rather strange. Its shape is only vaguely discernable in the darkness, but it is positioned so centrally within the picture that it can hardly escape the observer's attention. Whether van Gogh wanted to lend a morbid quality to the hedonistic activities going on at the café by means of the sinister vehicle remains purely speculative.

Completed a short time earlier, *The Night Café in the Place Lamartine in Arles*, (illus. pp. 140–141) an interior of another nighttime establishment, is a different story. In a letter to Theo, Vincent stated the course of action he was following with this painting. "In my picture of the night café, I have tried to express that the café is a place where a person could ruin himself, where he could go insane and commit a crime." Contrasting color effects are also integral in this work. "By

▷ *Café Terrace on the Place du Forum, Arles, at Night*, 1888,
oil on canvas, 31¾ x 25¾ in (80.7 x 65.3 cm),
Otterlo, Kröller-Müller Museum

Pages 140–141
The Night Café in the Place Lamartine in Arles, 1888,
watercolor, 17½ x 24¾ in (44.4 x 63.2 cm),
Bern, collection of Dr. Hans R. Hahnloser

Émile Bernard *Self-Portrait with Portrait of Gauguin*, 1888, oil on canvas, 18⅓ x 21¾ in (46.5 x 55.5 cm), Amsterdam, Van Gogh Museum

▷ **Paul Gauguin** *Self-Portrait with Portrait of Bernard* (*Les Misérables*), 1888, oil on canvas, 17¾ x 21⅔ in (45 x 55 cm), Amsterdam, Van Gogh Museum

means of the opposition of delicate pink, blood red, and dark red, of placid Louis XV and Veronese green against the yellow-green and hard, blue-green tones . . . all of this in an atmosphere of a hellish, blazing oven and pale yellow brimstone—I wanted to express the dark power of a tavern." [534] Vincent stressed the dangerous allure of the café in the same way he had in *Café Terrace on the Place du Forum, Arles, at Night,* by means of an alienating perspective that directs the observer's gaze into the depths of the composition.

Interestingly, Vincent established a link between *The Night Café* and *The Potato Eaters,* telling Theo they were on a par, "even if different." [533] Not only is their coloring entirely different, but to a certain extent, the two pictures form a pair of opposites. Their only common feature seems to consist of a table with light shining on it from a ceiling lamp that, in each

case, occupies the center of the pictorial space. Whereas *The Potato Eaters* depicts a family gathered peacefully around the dining table to share a paltry meal by the light of an oil lamp, a lone billiard table stands in the center of *The Night Café.* The dimensions and powerful contours of the room make it seem like a powerful symbol of idleness, of existence devoid of meaning—an allegory for a god-forsaken society that cannot develop any sort of integrative energy. Whether alone or in pairs, the people seem to be pulled apart by an unseen force, and they sit isolated from one another by the walls of the café which, significantly, are lit by four huge lamps. The strays, the lonely, and the uprooted appear not to find one another in this sad hideaway. The fascination with nightlife expressed by so many of his contemporaries in their works seems to be entirely absent from this famous painting by van Gogh.

STUDIO OF THE SOUTH

In the course of the year, van Gogh was able to at least partially integrate himself into Arles society. He had a small circle of friends and acquaintances, even if most of them, like Vincent himself, were from elsewhere and would stay in the vicinity of Arles only for a short while. He also had favorite haunts and established routines that formed the basis of his daily life. Nonetheless, van Gogh's letters clearly express how imperfect and incomplete he felt his own life to be. He wrote to Bernard, for example, that he lived like a monk who went to a bordello every fourteen days. "It's not very poetic, but I consider it my duty to subordinate my life to painting." [B 8] He put it more drastically to Theo that he painted "with self-denial, self-abdication, and a broken heart," for he was carrying out a "halfway voluntary, halfway enforced obliteration of his own life." [514] It seems obvious that Vincent was appealing to his brother for understanding, as Theo continued to

be a steadfast source of financial support. In any case, the comment sheds light on how extensively Vincent's maniacal work habits were driven by past traumas and self-hatred. "I feel," he wrote in another letter to Theo that fall, "that I must create to the point of spiritual annihilation and total physical emptiness." [557] As in the period he spent in Borinage, this preacher's son apparently believed that only self-sacrifice could give meaning to his existence and justify his brother's financial outlays. Even under the sun of southern France, van Gogh was not able to free himself of what had molded him in his homeland.

In Arles, art finally consumed van Gogh's entire life. Even when he had left Paris to go to Provence, he in no way saw this as a withdrawal. He had a loyal "agent" in the capital in his brother. Theo not only provided him with information about the latest developments in the art world, but was actually able to ensure that two of his brother's paintings, *Irises* and *Starry Night over the Rhone*, were represented in

◁ *Self-Portrait (Dedicated to Paul Gauguin)*, 1889, oil on canvas, 23½ x 19 in (59.5 x 48.3 cm), Cambridge, MA, Fogg Art Museum, Harvard University

Paul Gauguin *Van Gogh Painting Sunflowers*, 1888, oil on canvas, 28¾ x 35¾ in (73 x 91 cm), Amsterdam, Van Gogh Museum

the 1889 Salon des Indépendants. As he had done previously, Vincent also stayed up to date by reading trade journals, and he corresponded regularly with artist friends from his Paris days, especially with Bernard, who went to Brittany in the summer to work jointly with Gauguin. The exchange of ideas with both men is reflected in the work van Gogh produced that year in a variety of ways, in *The Sower*, for example, or the portraits with imagined backgrounds, and several two-dimensional compositions with strong contours that imply cloisonnistic inspiration.

The self-portraits that Bernard, Gauguin, their painter friend Charles Laval, and van Gogh exchanged with one another at Vincent's urging also attest to close contact between the artists. Van Gogh painted a portrait of himself as a "Buddhist monk" for Gauguin, a portrayal that resembles his painting of his friend Eugène Boch (illus. p. 137), and not

only because of the shaved head and close-cropped beard. There is also the intimation of a halo around Vincent's head, and there is a powerful flow painted in vague, concentric circles in the blue background, the focal point of which is located in the artist's right eye (illus. opposite). "I may arguably be permitted," Vincent wrote to Theo, in addition, "to enhance my personality in a portrait." [545] Admittedly, he had already surrounded his visage with aureoles in several Parisian self-portraits, thereby stylizing himself as an auratic artist. However much van Gogh was repeatedly shaken by self-doubt, there is nonetheless ample evidence of marked self-confidence.

Vincent's artistic outreach to his friends was connected to a more far-reaching plan. He nurtured the dream of an artists' cooperative, a "studio of the south." By his own admission, this plan had less to do with his personal ambitions as an

Vincent's House in Arles (The Yellow House), 1888, oil on canvas, 28⅓ x 36 in (72 x 91.5 cm), Amsterdam, Van Gogh Museum

▷ *Vincent's Bedroom in Arles*, 1888, oil on canvas, 38⅓ x 35¾ in (72 x 90 cm), Amsterdam, Van Gogh Museum

artist and more to do with his missionary zeal. "I would be truly satisfied," he wrote to his brother with a characteristic combination of modesty and conviction, "to be nothing more than a pathfinder for future painters who will work in the south." [519]

In fact, van Gogh put tremendous energy into making this project a reality. In May of 1889, he had already rented several rooms in a house on the Place Lamartine, which he first used as a storehouse for paintings and as a provisional (and primitive) workplace. His intention to set up an apartment and studio for two people fell through at first, due to the prohibitive costs. Only when his Uncle Cent died, on July 28, did the situation change. Vincent was not actually remembered in the wealthy art dealer's last will and testament. But Theo, who was the designated heir, sent his brother a share of the inheritance. Vincent was thereby in a position to have the Yellow House painted both inside

and out, and to furnish it initially with the most basic items. In September, Vincent moved into his new dwelling.

Two of his paintings from this period give a sense of the building, as well as the feelings and ideas that he associated with it. One shows the Yellow House (illus. above) from the vantage point of the Place Lamartine with a view of the Avenue de Montmajour, which van Gogh often took when he hiked around the surrounding areas on foot. The right half of the house, in which Vincent lived, is exactly in the center of the picture. Yet the building not only stands out due to its positioning, but also because of its bright yellow paint and the black windows with green shutters, which effectively put a face on the facade. The picture is characterized by yellow and blue contrasts, as are so many of van Gogh's works from the Arles period. On the one hand, the house catches the viewer's eye as a sparkling centerpiece; on the other, the dark window openings draw attention to the interior. Whereas the other buildings are sealed off with curtains, blinds, and window shutters, the Yellow House meets the observer's eye in a quasi-open way. It looks both cozy and inviting. Thus, the picture can also definitely be interpreted as an advertisement for Vincent's "studio of the south." And the clearly identifiable railway that ran atop the arch over the avenue might silently send the message to his artist friends that Arles was indeed connected to civilization.

As a matter of fact, van Gogh hoped his house would develop into an "outpost" or, at the very least, a "whistle stop" [599] for artists on their way to the tropics. For it was in the tropics, the ideal south, that he envisioned the future of painting.

The second picture provides a glimpse into van Gogh's bedroom (illus. below), which was hidden behind partially open green window shutters on the second floor. In terms of the portrayal of depth and the large bed, the composition resembles *The Night Café* with its massive billiard table. But Vincent's intention was certainly diametrically opposed to

that of the previous work. "Since I enhance the style by means of simplification," he explained in a letter to his brother, "the thought of peace, or broadly speaking, of sleep should cross a person's mind. In short, a glance at the picture should calm the mind or, more precisely, the imagination." [554]

To achieve this, van Gogh again used the full spectrum of primary colors, which he balanced harmoniously. He later reported to Theo that he had applied them flatly and simply, as in Japanese prints. "The walls are pale violet. The floor has red tiles. The wooden bed and chair are in the yellow of fresh butter; the sheets and pillows a very pale lime green. The bedspread is scarlet red. The window, green. The washstand is orange; the washbasin, blue. The doors, lilac. And that's about it—there is nothing else in this room with the closed shutters. Now the absolute earthiness of the furniture must still express the imperturbable sense of peace." [554] Two portraits, a landscape, and two other vaguely sketched pictures, presumably prints that hung decoratively on the walls, complete the furnishings. They are oriented around the

commanding bed, which, in this painting, Vincent apparently staged as the heart of his new home.

The Yellow House, however, was meant to be more than a simple accommodation and artists' workshop. Van Gogh's letters, in which he described the progress of his arrangements and sketched out his ideas, document his far-reaching goals. "From now on, you may consider yourself the owner of a country house in Arles, because I am eager to set it up so that it will please you, and so that it will become a studio of exceptional character," he reported enthusiastically, which, in light of the agonizing lines about himself that he had delivered to Theo during those months, may be astonishing. "I want to make a real artists' house out of it, nothing precious, certainly not that, absolutely not precious. But everything in it, from chairs to pictures, must have character." [534] Apparently what Vincent had in mind was no less than to create an all-around work of art that would integrate his paintings in an ideal way.

WAITING FOR GAUGUIN

In the course of the summer, Gauguin became the favored candidate on van Gogh's wish list for the cooperative studio. The two had not been more than fleeting acquaintances in Paris, but the spirited and widely traveled painter had made a big impression on van Gogh, both as an artist and as a person. When van Gogh learned that Gauguin was suffering from financial and health problems in Pont-Aven, he recognized his chance to lure him to Arles. He offered Gaugin the opportunity to work in the Yellow House, to live there, and to pay his way by giving Theo one painting per month, for which he would receive an additional stipend of 150 francs.

The very high hopes that van Gogh attached to the visit of his artist friend whom he so greatly admired is evident in his letters to Theo. In them, he discussed the topic extensively for months, which suggests just how anxious Vincent was that Gauguin might reject his offer. For his part, Gaugin held himself at a distance from the willful Dutchman's persistent enticements. But since Gauguin's situation did not improve, and because he was highly interested in building his relationship with Vincent's art-dealing brother, who had already exhibited some of his paintings, after a long delay he finally announced that he would indeed come to Arles at the end of October.

The prospect of Gauguin's visit provided new impetus for van Gogh's artistic production. "I'm now painting with

The Green Vineyard, 1888,
oil on canvas, 28½ x 36⅓ in (72.2 x 92.2 cm),
Otterlo, Kröller-Müller Museum

the wild enthusiasm of a person from Marseilles eating his bouillabaisse," he reported to Theo in August [526]. In mid-October, Vincent sent his brother a list of fifteen paintings that were intended for decorating the house [552]. In addition to *The Night Café, Starry Night,* and *The Yellow House* there are two works with seasonal motifs from the realm of agriculture, *The Green Vineyard* and *The Ploughed Field*; two works that show industrialized Arles, *The Railway Bridge over Avenue Montmajour, Arles* and *The Bridge at Trinquetaille* (illus. below); as well as *Tarascon Diligence* (illus. opposite), a work whose color scheme evokes the Provençal complexion of the town; and finally, five garden paintings with views of the park in Arles, which stretched out right in front of van Gogh's house. Among these latter pictures are three paintings in a cycle that Vincent called *The Poet's Garden*, which he

dedicated to Gauguin, whom he flatteringly dubbed the new poet of the south.

The variety of motifs as well as the outstanding quality of the paintings included in this group suggest that van Gogh did not intend to simply decorate his house beautifully. He undoubtedly wanted to impress Gauguin with his daring artistic feats. He wanted to be ready for the arrival of an artist he held in high regard, and whose judgment he most certainly feared. He also wanted to be of equal stature with the master, even if he had chosen Gauguin as head of his longed-for "studio of the south." So it was surely not for aesthetic reasons alone that, in addition to the garden paintings, van Gogh intended to hang in Gaugin's bedroom a series of works that are today considered his most famous paintings: the *Sunflowers* (illus. pp. 152–153).

The Bridge at Trinquetaille, 1888,
oil on canvas, 28½ x 36 in (72.5 x 91.5 cm),
New York, S. Kramarsky Collection

▷ *Tarascon Diligence,* 1888, oil on canvas,
28⅓ x 36¼ in (72 x 92 cm), Princeton, NJ, Henry and Rose Pearlman
Foundation, on long-term loan to Princeton University Art Museum

SUNFLOWERS

"In the room that either you or Gauguin will sleep in, if he comes, I want to cover the white walls with nothing but large yellow sunflowers. Whenever someone opens the window in the early morning, he will have a view of the green gardens, the rising sun, and the first houses in town. And then you'll see these large pictures with bunches of twelve or fourteen sunflowers that, along with a pretty bed, will fill this little room." [534] These lines to Theo document the paramount importance of the sunflower pictures to Vincent's concept of the Yellow House. They would bring not only the southern light inside the house, but also its inspiring energy.

Compared with his Parisian *Two Cut Sunflowers* (illus. p. 105), the ones he painted in Arles in August 1888 were more ambitious, because van Gogh painted them from fresh flowers rather than from dried ones. "I work every morning from sunrise onward," he reported to Theo, "for flowers fade quickly, and the entire thing must be painted in one session." [526] The sunflowers also gave Vincent an opportunity to display his craftsmanship. The convincing portrayal of

readily perishable objects, such as flowers or fruit, had been a hallmark of artistic ability in painting still lifes since baroque times. Most importantly, the motif fit into van Gogh's drive for spontaneity. It was his declared ideal to complete a work "in one session," because he believed that life—emotionally experienced reality—could be more immediately captured on canvas in this way. The astounding tempo at which van Gogh worked can best be explained by a combination of the Protestant work ethic of the pastor's son, inner restlessness, and the desire to approximate the physical endurance of the peasantry by wearing himself out. For Vincent, speed in painting was also an expression of his search for truth. Since he painted the sunflower pictures from fresh flowers, he was admittedly unable to realize his original plan to create a dozen paintings. "I had wanted to paint more sunflowers," he informed his brother in September, crestfallen, "but there were no more available." [543]

Van Gogh seems to have wanted to test the limits of his capacity with the sunflower paintings, because he increased the number of flowers with each picture. At first he painted a group of three, then five, and finally twelve and fifteen

Still Life: Vase with Twelve Sunflowers, 1888,
oil on canvas, 36¼ x 28¾ in (92 x 73 cm),
Munich, Bavarian State Art Collections, Neue Pinakothek

Still Life: Vase with Fifteen Sunflowers, 1888,
oil on canvas, 36¼ x 28¾ in (92 x 73 cm),
London, National Gallery

Les Alyscamps, 1888, oil on canvas,
36¼ x 29 in (92 x 73.7 cm), private collection

sunflowers. These final two works are the core of the series, and constitute the "real" van Gogh sunflower paintings. In January 1890, van Gogh used them as models for additional still lifes.

In their conception, the sunflower paintings are entirely tailored to the appearance of the flowers, which are composed of incredibly varied yellow tones, and van Gogh's impasto style renders an extraordinarily lively surface. The contrasting background and base have been reduced to colored surfaces

Van Gogh's original vision for the sunflower pictures was a "symphony in blue and yellow," a hymn to summer and sunshine. But blue occupies a larger area in just one of the two major works in the series. While the still life with fifteen flowers (illus. p. 153) consists almost exclusively of various shades of yellow—they carry over from the flowers to the vase, base, and background—the yellow flowers in the other painting are in striking contrast with their bright blue background, which in turn is associated with the blue of the

Les Alyscamps: Falling Autumn Leaves, 1888, oil on canvas, 28⅔ x 36¼ in (72.8 x 91.9 cm), Otterlo, Kröller-Müller Museum

whose only texture derives from the thick application of oil paints, and their arrangement in space is only discernable by dint of a horizontal line. The powerfully contoured Provençal vase has returned, its depth barely developed, from which sunflowers appear to erupt with elemental force in a widely fanned-out bouquet.

sky, emphasizing the symbolic meaning of the motif all the more clearly. The "rustic" sunflowers in both still lifes, as well as van Gogh's later versions depicting various stages of the flowers' growth, can be understood as a metaphor for the cycle of nature. In his humble worship of the creation, Vincent himself simply called it a symbol for "thankfulness." [W 20]

Memory of the Garden at Etten, 1888, oil on canvas,
29 x 36½ in (73.5 x 92.5 cm), St. Petersburg, Hermitage Museum

The enduring popularity of the *Sunflower* paintings, as well as their significance as key works of modern art, certainly rests less upon these various levels of interpretation and more on their immediate expressiveness. In the interplay of color composition, technique, and pictorial format, van Gogh attained a level of expression that was previously unknown not only within the floral still life genre, but in fact must be regarded as groundbreaking in the development of painting as a whole. Like almost no other work, the *Sunflowers* represent an art form in which the creative subject stands at the center and sheds light on its being and unique relationship to the world.

It is generally thought that the explosive element contained in these pictures is probably the reason that, over time, the *Sunflower* paintings became synonymous with the sort of artistic passion that eventually consumed van Gogh. This view can also be borne out by the placement of the artist's signature on the vase, as though the container would represent his person and the sunflower bouquet his work. Van Gogh seems to have sensed the importance of this series of pictures for the acceptance of his work as a whole. "You know, of course," he wrote to Theo, "that the peony belongs to Jeannin, the hollyhock to Quost, and the sunflower to me." [573]

◁ *Portrait of the Artist's Mother,* 1888,
oil on canvas, 16 x 12¾ in (40.5 x 32.5 cm),
Pasadena, Norton Simon Art Foundation

Paul Gauguin *Night Café at Arles (Madame Ginoux)*, 1888,
oil on canvas, 28¾ x 36¼ in (73 x 92 cm), Moscow, Pushkin Museum

▷ *L'Arlésienne (Madame Ginoux)*, 1888, oil on canvas,
35½ x 28⅓ in (90 x 72 cm), New York, Metropolitan Museum of Art

GAUGUIN IN ARLES

Gauguin arrived in Arles early in the morning of October 23, 1888. He moved into the Yellow House that same day. Very few letters by either artist are still extant from the nine-week period that he spent there with van Gogh. Surely the tragic ending has had a lasting effect on the retrospective view of their now-famous workshop and artists' living quarters. Although the idea of a more-or-less constant state of emergency is certainly exaggerated, Gauguin and van Gogh undoubtedly experienced a time that was characterized by tremendous intensity on both the creative and emotional planes. The meeting of these artists was ill-fated from the very beginning. In the weeks prior to Gaugin's arrival, Vincent had worked intensely, burnt himself out, and suffered from acute self-doubt. He had only gradually recovered from the

repercussions of another bout of dysentery. Furthermore, he attached extraordinarily high hopes to Gauguin's arrival. And Gauguin, unlike the pastor's son from Brabant, hardly expected that the southern French city in Provence would inspire him to any great extent, given that he had lived for four years in Lima, Peru as a child and had later traveled the seas. He longed for the genuine tropics that he had visited with Laval the year before. He hoped that, with Theo's help, he would be able to save enough money from the sale of his paintings to be able to return to Martinique. For him, Arles was merely an interim solution.

Other factors made the meeting between a hypersensitive host and his detached, dominating guest fraught with difficulty. The two not only had seemingly opposite temperaments, but also distinctly different artistic concepts and ways of working. Gauguin considered van Gogh's

impulsive way of painting suspect. As he saw it, impasto style left too much room for happenstance, as did painting directly before a subject. Gauguin's synthesism abstracted sensory reality through imagination and recollection, and was anything but spontaneous in origin. The esoteric play of form and color that infuses his works was the result of a creative process that demanded a great deal of control and concentration. And it took time, as well.

Van Gogh was surely aware of these differences, and they made him feel insecure. "I never work from my intellect," he emphasized in a letter to Bernard written shortly before Gauguin's arrival. "Others may be more talented at fantasy studies, and you could certainly be one of them, as is Gauguin . . . maybe I could, too, when I am old. But until that time, I will constantly devour nature. I am exaggerating, for I do sometimes alter a motif. But I do not invent the entire picture; quite the contrary. I find it already complete in nature, but it must be unravelled." [B 19]

Nonetheless, the artists' cooperative seems to have begun on an entirely auspicious note. Vincent introduced Gauguin to the city and showed him the surrounding areas. Through a pragmatism born of necessity, Gauguin not only understood how to bring order to a household, but a certain degree of comfort and coziness as well. And van Gogh, with his compulsively ascetic character, would never have been able to realize these things on his own. They worked together in the open air. They sometimes brought models into the studio—such as the Ginouxs, an innkeeper couple with whom Vincent had lived until September—and painted their portraits simultaneously (illus. pp. 158–159). To save money, they cooked and ate at home, and henceforth stretched their own canvases. Gauguin bought twenty meters of "very strong" canvas for this purpose, as Vincent remarked to Theo. What makes this interesting is that the coarse fabric was quite unsuited to van Gogh's impasto application.

Gauguin took on the leading role, as was intended, and at first van Gogh was apparently willing to follow him. They worked together in Les Alyscamps, the ancient Roman necropolis near Arles. Vincent made a series of four oil paintings there that would indicate some movement toward his friend's ideas. Two of the paintings show the avenue lined with poplars in fall colors (illus. p. 154), a perspective that can also be found in van Gogh's early works. For the version of *Les Alyscamps* that he apparently completed somewhat later on (illus. p. 155), he chose to position himself above and outside the *allée* so that the narrow trees along the avenue are cut off at the top edge of the picture and also partially at the bottom.

The Sower, 1888,
oil on burlap and canvas,
12¾ x 36⅔ in (73.5 x 93 cm),
Zurich, E. G. Bührle Foundation

Portrait of Armand Roulin, 1888,
oil on canvas, 25½ x 21¼ in (65 x 54 cm),
Rotterdam, Boijmans Van Beuningen Museum

▷ *Camille Roulin,* 1888,
oil on canvas, 17 x 13¾ in (43.2 x 34.9 cm),
Philadelphia, Philadelphia Museum of Art

As a result, the rows of tree trunks pervade the painting in the form of strong, vertical lines. This lends the composition an almost graphic character that is both reminiscent of Gauguin's works and of Japanese color woodblock prints, an art form revered by both artists. The powerful contours and thin, two-dimensional color application also reveal cloisonnistic inspiration.

Animated by Gauguin, van Gogh tried to allow more room for imagination. From memory, he painted a packed dance hall, the spectators at a bullfight in the arena, and a "red vineyard" that he and Gauguin had seen earlier on one of their walks.

While Vincent was quite happy with the results of these last-mentioned mnemonic works, he was certainly moving on familiar terrain here in terms of subject matter. However, he apparently found it more difficult to paint entirely "according to fantasy." The painting *Memory of the Garden at Etten* (illus. p. 157), a rather unconvincing experiment in which he blended the portrayal of the Place Lamartine with memories of Holland, was his clearest attempt to try out Gauguin's ideas. One of the three female figures resembles Madame Ginoux, while the older woman next to her is thought to represent Vincent's mother, as the *Portrait of the Artist's Mother* (illus. p. 156) would suggest. Van Gogh had painted the latter from a photograph a short time earlier.

Apparently van Gogh felt a need to explain to his sister, Wil, why he objected so emphatically to any visible realism in this garden painting. He wrote to her that he had wanted to reproduce the poetic character and style of the garden as he experienced it. "Let us assume for now that the women walking there were you and our mother; let's even suppose that neither bears any, not even the slightest, generic, empty resemblance to either of you—to me, the deliberate choice of colors, the dark violet, animated by the lemon yellow of the dahlias, expresses mother's personality." Likewise, "the bizarre, affected, and repeated lines," were meant to portray the garden, "as in a dream . . . at once, in its true character, yet stranger than reality." [W 9] Vincent's formulations sound unusually vague, so much so that despite the intimacy of the theme, it is almost as if his own work remained foreign to him. And this foreignness seems to have rubbed off on the painting itself. In borrowing from the pointillistic, dotted style that Gauguin had rejected, Vincent appears to have wanted to defiantly prove his artistic independence, after all.

By contrast, van Gogh achieved more felicitous results with two other "fantasy" pieces. In November, he once again returned to the sower motif. Two versions emerged, the smaller of which presumably served as a preliminary study, and is now housed in the Van Gogh Museum in Amsterdam (the larger of the two is illustrated on pp. 160–161). Both oil paintings, which significantly differ from one another only in their dimensions, show a palpable connection to Gauguin and the Japanese masters, most especially in the truncated tree that diagonally crosses the foreground of the composition. Yet the composition looks distinctive. As compared with his earlier depictions, the figure of the sower approaches the viewer more closely in these renditions. The actions of the faceless figure seem at once solemn and intimate, and the glowing, golden disk of the setting sun soars above his head like a powerful halo.

As in the sower paintings van Gogh had made the previous summer, this picture also emphasizes the symbolism of the motif. But here, the cyclical moment has been expressed differently and more subtly. The color scheme suggests the change of seasons and the transition from day to night, and the dynamic composition makes the changeability of the situation perceptible, yet also forms a harmonious whole. Astoundingly, in this studio work Vincent achieved his most convincing realization of the sower theme, a subject of central importance to him.

▷ *Paul Gauguin's Armchair*, 1888, oil on canvas,
35⅔ x 28½ in (90.5 x 72.5 cm), Amsterdam, Van Gogh Museum

◁ *Vincent's Chair with His Pipe*, 1888, oil on canvas,
36⅔ x 29 in (93 x 73.5 cm), London, National Gallery

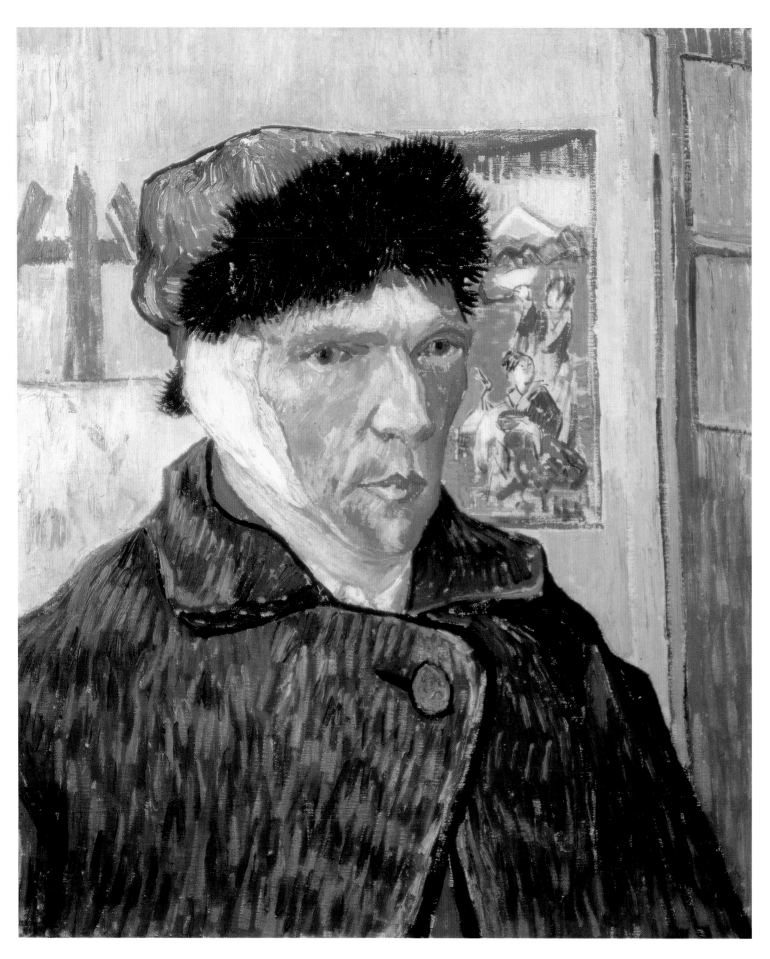

Self-Portrait with Bandaged Ear, 1889, oil on canvas,
23⅔ x 19¼ in (60 x 49 cm), London, Courtauld Institute Galleries

In the end, however, working from memory remained foreign to van Gogh's nature. Although he assured Theo that he "did not unwillingly paint from memory," [560] he began a series of portraits of the Roulin family in November, among them the *Portrait of Armand Roulin*, as well as that of *Camille Roulin* (illus. pp. 162–163). This return to painting from models did not constitute a complete about-face, because Vincent also tried to continue working from his imagination in the style of Gauguin. But this turn of events could be taken as a sign that neither a functional, mutually beneficial working relationship nor the teacher-student relationship that Gauguin may have envisioned had developed between the two artists.

In the end, then, three paintings that at first glance might appear to express a bond between Gauguin and van Gogh serve more as an explicit commentary on their prevailing differences. Gauguin's portrait of van Gogh, which shows Vincent painting sunflowers (illus. p. 145), has actually been construed by some interpreters as a criticism of van Gogh's painting for being much too fixated on immediate, visible reality. This view may be confirmed by Gauguin's contention that van Gogh ought to have recognized himself in the picture for the lunatic he was. The famous pair of symbolic portraits, *Vincent's Chair with His Pipe* and *Paul Gauguin's Armchair* (illus. pp. 164–165), look melancholy from today's perspective, because the empty, unoccupied chairs seem to foreshadow the end of the cooperative. And the contrasting compositions of the paintings point, above all, to the fundamental differences between the artists.

Letters written by both artists also testify to the ever more forceful clash between their different positions. Gauguin told Bernard that, in matters of painting, he and van Gogh hardly agreed on a single point. "He is romantic, and I tend more toward the primitive," he stated categorically, having previously held forth about van Gogh's inflexibility and dogmatism. In mid-December, Gauguin finally informed Theo by letter that he would be leaving Arles shortly, because he considered a peaceful coexistence with Vincent impossible. Shortly thereafter, he revised his decision, but no genuine improvement in the situation had occurred.

After Gauguin and van Gogh had visited the Musée Fabre in Montpelier, which was famous for its extensive collections of historic and modern art, Vincent wrote to his brother about exhausting discussions that were charged with "extraordinarily electric tension." [564] In another letter, dated December 23, he wrote, disillusioned, "I believe that Gauguin has had enough of the good city of Arles, the little yellow house in which we work and, above all, of me." Reportedly, Gauguin would soon decide whether to depart or to stay. "I am waiting for his decision with complete equanimity!" [565] The situation must have escalated on that same day.

CATASTROPHE

It is not possible to precisely reconstruct what befell Vincent van Gogh on that fateful pre-Christmas evening of 1888. Whether due to shame or because he did not want to remember them, he did not shed any light on the incidents, which remain shrouded in legend. The authoritative sources are thus restricted to three: a short announcement in the local newspaper, Gauguin's verbal account as conveyed by Bernard, and Gauguin's memories from many years later, in which he, a long-since famous painter, was visibly at pains to appear in the best possible light.

What is known for certain is that on the evening in question van Gogh used a razor to cut off the lower portion of his own left ear, then took it to a brothel afterward. The following morning, the police broke into the Yellow House and found Vincent, weakened by considerable blood loss and unconscious in bed, and they immediately took him to the hospital. The statements that Vincent chased after Gauguin in the park and supposedly threatened him with the razor before mutilating himself come solely from Gaugin, who claimed to have spent the night in a hotel.

To this day, it remains unclear who actually instigated the deed. The question of whether it marked the onset of van Gogh's mental illness remains unanswerable, as there are indications of earlier "spells" ("attacks"). There is also uncertainty about the type of illness that would manifest at irregular intervals in more-or-less acute outbreaks of mental derangement during the remaining nineteen months of van Gogh's life. While Vincent himself believed he was suffering from epilepsy, which accords with the opinion of his physician, Dr. Felix Rey (illus. p. 169), today there is some concensus thought that van Gogh likely suffered from bipolar disorder, which could have been worsened by poor nutrition, work-related stress, and excessive consumption of tobacco and alcohol.

As dramatic as the incidents of December 23, 1889 may have seemed, developments in the weeks that followed were equally uneventful. Having been notified by Gauguin, Theo hurried to Arles by train to personally assess his brother's condition and to take care of the most urgent matters. Shortly before the trip, Theo had become engaged to Johanna Bonger, the sister of a Dutch friend.

He departed from Arles again two days later, presumably in the company of Gauguin. Vincent was apparently no longer hovering on the brink of death. Furthermore, it must have reassured Theo that he was able to gain the consent of the local evangelical pastor, Frédéric Salle, to look after his brother. Joseph Roulin and Madame Ginoux also visited Vincent, whose condition quickly improved so that he was already able to move back into his house on January 7. Once there, he immediately went back to work.

Portrait of Joseph Roulin, 1889, oil on canvas,
25⅓ x 21¾ in (64.4 x 55.2 cm), New York, Museum of Modern Art

Portrait of Doctor Felix Rey, 1889, oil on canvas,
25¼ x 20¾ in (64 x 53 cm), Moscow, Pushkin Museum

LA BERCEUSE—WOMAN ROCKING A CRADLE

Apparently, van Gogh's main concern was to return to normalcy. He actually recorded the results of his "accident" in two self-portraits that show him with a bandaged ear (illus. p. 2, p. 166). However, it would be difficult to substantiate any break in his work during January and February 1889. Vincent resumed work on a portrait of Madame Roulin as *La Berceuse* (literally, "cradle song"; illus. opposite) that he had started before Christmas. There are a total of five slightly different versions of the portrait, all of which originated between December and the end of March. They constitute the highpoint in a series of portraits van Gogh painted of the Roulin family, along with three half-length portraits of Mr. Roulin (illus. p. 168), Vincent's postmaster friend, which he completed in April.

The apparent tenderness expressed in this wonderful series of portraits conveys the gratitude van Gogh felt toward the family, especially toward his dear friend, Joseph Roulin. At the same time, the series is the clearest expression of the democratic spirit in his art. It was considered the privilege of the ruling class and wealthy merchants to immortalize themselves and their families in portrait paintings. Yet, in this case, van Gogh portrayed simple folk, the family of a dyed-in-the-wool republican.

In *La Berceuse* van Gogh took up a classic theme of genre painting, but by placing the cradle outside the picture he transformed it into something highly original. Only a cord in the mother's hands provides a link to the baby's tiny bed. The braided cord runs from the cradle rocker's lap to the lower edge of the painting toward the viewer, who thus sees from the position of the child. This is a melancholy work that expresses the longing for familial warmth. Vincent told his brother that it was inspired by a conversation with Gauguin. The two had been discussing the difficult and lonely life of Icelandic fishermen. The picture was intended to communicate to the sailors in their bunks at sea a feeling that "they were hearing their own lullaby again." [574] The meaningful elements in van Gogh's painting—a sense of relationship and the offering of solace—clearly emerge in this statement. To Vincent, the boat was a cradle, and the sea was a metaphor for the world. Just as the child in the cradle trusts in its mother's care, the seaman should also feel a divine presence in the waves. For he, like the peasant, was the embodiment of the simple, hardworking man.

Striking is the pattern in the background, which resembles floral wallpaper. It not only surrounds Madame Roulin, its shapes and colors also refer to the mother, who assumes a dignified pose, seated in a simple chair. The pattern winds around the woman like an ornament, as if an auratic energy were emanating from her. Van Gogh used this pattern in a similar fashion for his portraits of Dr. Rey and Joseph Roulin

(illus. pp. 168–169). With it, he also showed reverence for Bernard and Gauguin, since he was familiar with similar backgrounds in their works. Even after Gauguin had left him, Vincent apparently aimed to expand his range of expression by adapting his symbolist colleague's ideas. The great importance van Gogh attached to *La Berceuse* is documented by the fact that he envisaged the portrait of Madame Roulin as the centerpiece of a triptych, surrounded by two sunflowers.

> *"I must tell you—and you can see it in the Berceuse, however much this weak attempt may have failed—if I'd had the strength to continue, I would have done natural portraits of holy men and women, and they would have seemed like something from another century. They would have been taken from the present-day bourgeoisie, and yet they would have had something in common with the early Christians."* [605]
>
> *Vincent van Gogh to Theo, September 10, 1889*

COLD SPRING

Although Van Gogh did not attain the same level of artistic productivity as had experienced before Gauguin's visit, he still worked continually. He concentrated mainly on still lifes, as he had in the wintertime. He also painted variations on both of the large summertime sunflower paintings, particularly since Gauguin had expressed the wish to trade a picture of his for one of those paintings. Van Gogh apparently placed great store in reconciling with Gauguin. Vincent's letters only occasionally reveal a grudge against his colleague, and many lines even hint at the hope that Gauguin would return to him in Arles. As a matter of fact, they would never see one another again.

Van Gogh gradually came to realize how illusory his desire for a revival of the artists' cooperative was. His growing disillusionment may have contributed to a relapse into illness in February 1889, from which he recovered only slowly. Plagued by insomnia, hallucinations, and delusions, he ended up in the hospital again. He returned home to the Yellow House within a short time, but suffered yet another

La Berceuse (Augustine Roulin), 1889,
oil on canvas, 35¾ x 28⅓ in (91 x 72 cm),
Otterlo, Kröller-Müller Museum

> "I hope it was a nothing more than simple artistic madness on my part, followed by a high fever resulting from extensive blood loss, since an artery was sliced through. But my appetite came back right away, my digestion is fine, and my blood (supply) is being replaced from day to day. My mind is also improving with each passing day" [569].
>
> Vincent van Gogh to Theo concerning his ear injury, January 7, 1889

severe blow in March. Thirty citizens of Arles successfully petitioned the mayor to confine Vincent to hospital, as he was ostensibly a danger to the general public, and the police locked up his house with all his pictures inside it. In a city where he had found friends like the Roulins, where he believed that he had largely been accepted, the community had now turned against him, the "ragged dog."

In spite of everything, van Gogh continued to work. He painted the dormitory and the hospital garden. And, as in the previous year, he captured the Provençal spring in wonderful pictures. But Vincent now saw the blooming landscape with greater aloofness. The colors look cooler, less radiant, and there is no longer a feeling of immediacy or of being overwhelmed in these works. One of the paintings even moves the observer into the position of a prisoner. It shows the blooming gardens of Arles through three poplar trunks that give the picture a powerful, vertical structure (illus. right). But unlike the trees in the Alyscamps pictures, these trunks look like bars. They block the observer's view of the countryside, upon which the panorama of the city weighs heavily in cold color combinations. Clearly, this work is an expression of the isolation van Gogh felt in those anguished days, and loneliness would define his everyday life to a much greater extent in the months that followed. After the Yellow House was impacted by a flood in April, Vincent decided to spend several weeks recovering in an asylum for the mentally ill near Saint-Rémy. In the end, he stayed there for a year. Ten years after his father had wanted to have him committed to an institution in Gheel, Vincent effectively took this step on his own.

Orchard in Blossom with View of Arles, 1889,
oil on canvas, 28⅓ x 36¼ in (72 x 92 cm),
Munich, Bavarian State Art Collections, Neue Pinakothek

VAN GOGH AND GAUGUIN

Vincent van Gogh achieved posthumous fame as a lonely painter, yet throughout his entire life, he had dreamed of being part of a united community of artists. In Arles, he tried to realize this vision by inviting Paul Gauguin to the Yellow House so that they could establish a "studio of the south" together. These two key figures of modern art lived under the same roof for two months, and then their tension-filled collaboration came to a tragic and legendary end.

Paul Gauguin, "a man about town,"
photograph, 1891

Like van Gogh, Gauguin began his artistic career relatively late in life. Also like his Dutch acquaintance, he was in dire financial straights and suffered from a lack of recognition for a very long time. Still, this was a meeting between two people of very different character: the Parisian-born offspring of a leftist, liberal family who grew up in Lima, Peru, without a father, and the pastor's son from Brabant whose family roots were always so important to him. Unlike the nervous, shy, ascetically inclined van Gogh, Gauguin came across as self-assured and confident, and was not at all averse to the finer things in life. Widely traveled, he was personally acquainted with the tropics, but he also knew about the amenities and limitations of bourgeois existence. As a husband and father

of five children, he had worked successfully as a stockbroker before he took up art as a profession, despite adamant opposition from his wife, who finally left him. From then on, he led an unstable life.

Van Gogh and Gauguin first met in the fall of 1886 in Paris, where Vincent's brother, Theo, an art dealer and advocate for the avant-garde, introduced them. At that time, Vincent had just begun to try out the impressionist way of painting from which Gauguin had already visibly distanced himself. They both agreed that the development of painting had in no way attained its limits with impressionism.

The two were apparently casual acquaintances at first. Since Gauguin started off on a six-month trip to Panama and Martinique in April 1887, they did not form a closer bond at that time. This makes it all the more amazing that, during the following summer, Vincent tried so vehemently to win Gauguin over as head of a cooperative studio. While van Gogh was in Arles, Gauguin, Émile Bernard, and several other artists had developed the concept of "synthetic" (symbolist) painting in the fishing village of Pont-Aven in Brittany.

Surely van Gogh's interest in Gauguin as an artist was crucial to his efforts. As a visionary, he was convinced that the future of painting lay in the south and that a return to the simple forms of folk art was indispensible to artistic renewal. But personal fascination with his older colleague may have also played a role. Whether the attraction was colored by homosexual feelings, as has sometimes been hypothesized, is open to question. For Gaugin, on the other hand, the financial aspect of van Gogh's offer was a decisive factor in his positive response to Vincent's coaxing, as is clear from the extant letters.

Regardless of how the studio alliance came about and what the circumstances were, their completely different artistic temperaments were undoubtedly reason enough for the relationship between Gauguin and van Gogh did not turn out to be a harmonious one. Alone the fact that Vincent was used to painting in an energetic impasto style, and finished his pictures in the shortest possible time, while Gauguin applied the paint thinly in a very controlled manner that required infinitely more time, must have put a strain on their workday routine. Even more difficult was that Gauguin's artistic approach remained foreign to van Gogh's nature. This was not because he rejected the idea of uniting outer reality with the inner world of the imagination through abstraction. Rather, he derived inspiration from reality as experienced through his senses. Gauguin's practice of painting from the imagination did not satisfy van Gogh.

Their differences proved to be irreconcilable, so much so that Vincent told his brother about discussions filled with "extraordinarily electric tension," while Gauguin declared in a letter to Theo that he and Vincent could not live together

According to Gauguin, the situation escalated one evening after van Gogh had thrown an absinthe glass at him in a tavern, whereupon Gaugin announced that he would be departing the following day. As he left the house to go for a walk, Vincent had followed him with a razor in his hand. Gaugin's powerful gaze had induced his friend to abandon his homicidal intentions and go back into the house. When Gauguin returned the next morning after spending the night in a guest house, he found a crowd of people in front of the Yellow House. Van Gogh had cut off "his ear right next to

Paul Gauguin *Old Women of Arles*, oil on canvas, 28¾ x 36¼ in (73 x 92 cm) Chicago, Art Institute of Chicago

peacefully because their dispositions were incompatible. Gauguin later wrote in his memoirs that a fight between van Gogh and himself had inevitably been brewing. ". . . one was a veritable volcano, and the other boiling inwardly . . . ." He then described the tragic ending of the artists' cooperative in similarly dramatic terms.

his head," wrapped it up and taken it to a prostitute in a brothel they frequented, and then returned home and fallen into a deep sleep. This, Gauguin's version of the events of December 23, 1888, is obviously rather freely rendered; it has been established that van Gogh cut off at most a piece of his lower left earlobe.

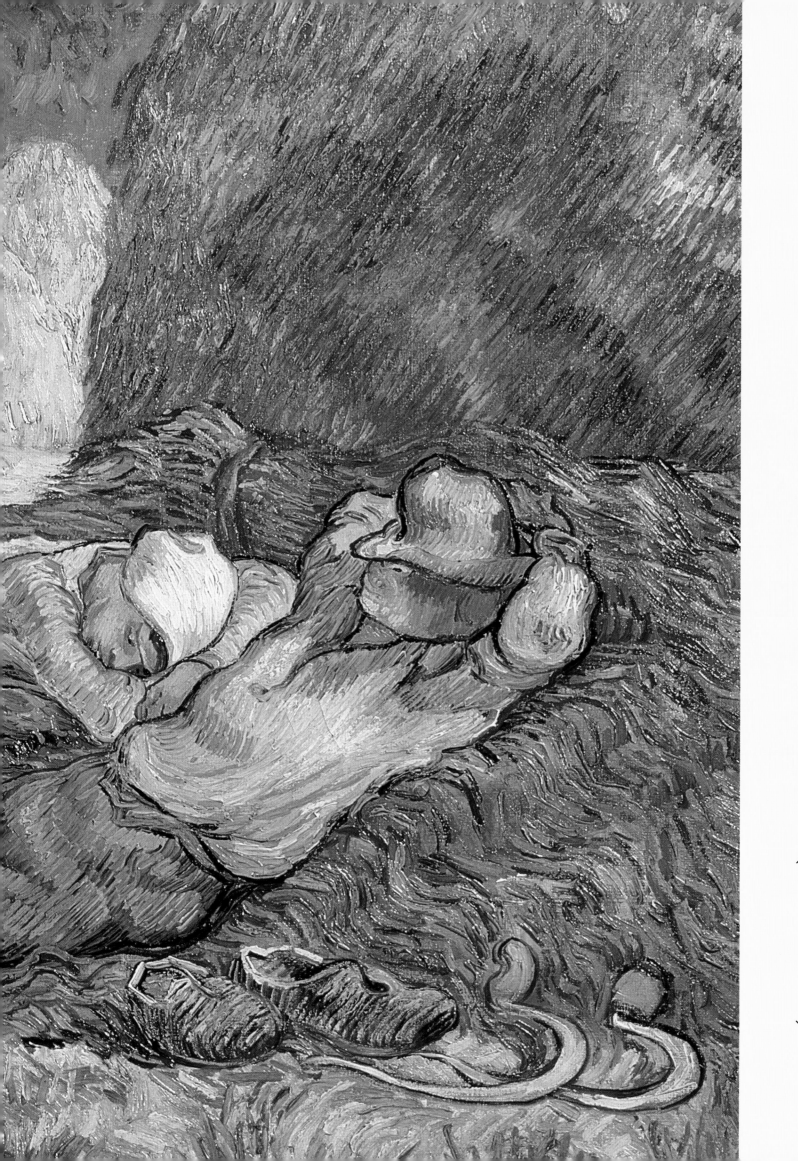

PAINTING IN LONELINESS: SAINT-RÉMY

Still Life: Vase with Irises, 1890, oil on canvas,
28¾ x 36½ in (73 x 93 cm), New York, Metropolitan Museum of Art

BEHIND WALLS

On May 8, 1889, van Gogh arrived in Saint-Rémy in the company of Pastor Salles. Unlike Arles, the little Provençal town approximately twenty miles away was surrounded by a charming Mediterranean landscape doted with pines, cypresses, and olive trees. Not far from the ruins of a Roman city, between the southern outskirts of town and the Alpilles mountain range that separates the region from the Rhone valley lowlands, lay the Saint-Paul-de-Mausole sanatorium. Originally a convent, Catholic nuns still worked at the facility, whose original purpose was evidenced by the cell-like sleeping quarters of the occupants, who were admitted there for every imaginable kind of psychological illness. Vincent, who kept his distance from the other patients, also moved into one of the cells.

Although he sought to recover in the seclusion of the convent, van Gogh soon began to work again. Since he was initially not permitted to leave the premises, he first painted in the clinic's overgrown garden. He immediately discovered several lovely motifs, among them irises, which were in full

bloom when he arrived. They inspired him to create one of his most famous flower paintings, the image of an abundant bed of irises (illus. pp. 180–181). The painting achieves extraordinary intensity from its dynamic composition and especially by means of the masterfully effective heightening of the color composition in the violet-blue flowers. The low perspective and, for a plein air painting, the unusual proximity to the subject are conspicuous. The observer is thus overcome by the sweep and vitality of the irises.

Just how deeply van Gogh's art was stimulated by direct experience and the felt presence of nature is once again evident here. In this regard, his art not only differs from the academic tradition, but also from works of symbolist fantasy. However much it reflects his fascination with Japanese art and his interest in decorative patterns, the iris image therefore serves as an indication that Vincent was at pains to more keenly differentiate himself from Gauguin's approach. Nonetheless, his former companion was a constant source of inspiration, and van Gogh still remained in contact with him through written correspondance.

Contrary to his original intentions, van Gogh stayed an entire year in Saint-Rémy, and thus experienced the irises in bloom there a second time. He captured them in two wonderful still lifes that are comparable in their conception to the sunflowers pictures from Arles (illus. pp. 178–179). Interestingly, the iris painting he completed shortly after his arrival shows a fine rendering of the floral structure similar to that of his later studio works. The sanatorium garden apparently made it possible for van Gogh to paint very peacefully and with great diligence outdoors.

The old cloister complex of Saint-Paul-de-Mausole actually offered certain advantages, despite the poor quality of

▷ *Still Life: Vase with Irises Against a Yellow Background*, 1890, oil on canvas, 36¼ x 29 in (92 x 73.5 cm), Amsterdam, Van Gogh Museum

Pages 176–177
Noon: Rest from Work (after Millet), detail, 1890, oil on canvas, 28¾ x 35¾ in (73 x 91 cm), Paris, Musée d'Orsay

the food and inadequate medical care. There was a second cell that van Gogh could use as a studio, and he was soon allowed to work outside the grounds of the facility. Under these conditions, the monotonous, regimented daily routine of the hospital must have had a genuinely positive effect on Vincent's creative energy, at least at the beginning. In his self-imposed isolation, art became his sole mission in life as never before. It became a therapy that was probably far more effective than the water baths that the clinic staff prescribed for him. Thus, despite several serious attacks that interrupted his work flow on several occasions, van Gogh was almost as productive during his twelve-month stay at the sanatorium as he was during his first year in Provence.

THE ENCLOSED FIELD

Nevertheless, van Gogh did not find the same diversity of subject matter in the quiet, secluded environs of Saint-Paule-de-Mausole, as expressed notably in the lack of people to serve as models. He concentrated on landscapes even more and only sporadically painted portraits. The serial character of his work from Saint-Rémy is also notable. Time and again van Gogh would take up the same motif, creating variations and new versions of recent as well as older paintings. Isolation definitely left its mark on his work, increasing the reflexive nature of his art.

A recurring motif during those months was the wheat field enclosed within the walls of the cloister complex, which van Gogh could see through the barred window of his room (illus. p. 184), "a vista à la Goyen," he wrote to Theo. "Above it, I see the sun rise in all its glory in the morning." [592] Van Gogh had captured the view from the window of whatever room he was living in at nearly every step along his artistic journey, but the enclosed field in front of the hills of Les Alpilles provided him with special inspiration. The harmony between agricultural work and eternal nature had always been a central theme in his work. In addition, the wall he saw from his window had a special allure. He let his particular situation in life flow into his pictures through it, and it allowed him to give concrete expression to his existential loneliness.

The best-known variation on this motif shows a peasant cutting ripe grain (illus. p. 183). Seeing the undulating wheat field, which was set onto the canvas in powerful impasto style, the reaper's undertakings look heroic, as if he were fighting against a luminous yellow sea. In a letter to his brother, Vincent described the man as "a nondescript figure who

Irises, 1889,
oil on canvas, 28 x 36½ in (71 x 93 cm),
Los Angeles, J. Paul Getty Museum

Field of Spring Wheat at Sunrise, 1889, oil on canvas,
29 x 36 in (73.5 x 91.5 cm), Otterlo, Kröller-Müller Museum

works like the devil in the blazing heat to finish his task." To him, the reaper was the counterpart of the sower, "a picture of death, in that men are like the grain that he is cutting down." But there was nothing sad in this death: "It happens in broad daylight, when everything is bathed in pure, golden light from the sun." [604]

Another obvious interpretation is to understand the reaper as a reference to van Gogh himself. In following this line of thought, the wheat field becomes a metaphor for his own artistic creation. Vincent seems to have felt that he had not yet attained his goals, for in the painting only a small part of the harvest has been brought in; the larger portion of the task still lay ahead of him, a thoroughly hopeful outlook. And, in fact, van Gogh went about his work tirelessly in Saint-Rémy, a lone reaper, separated from his own life by a wall.

CYPRESSES

During his time at the sanatorium, van Gogh became increasingly interested in a motif that he considered especially characteristic of the Provençal landscape. "I am constantly occupied with cypresses," he reported to Theo. "I would like to do something with them like I did with the sunflowers, because it surprises me that, so far, no one has painted them as I see them." [596] Within his spiritual worldview, Vincent apparently viewed the cypresses stretching toward the heavens as a sign of the paranormal in nature, an allegory for transcendence that distinctly reminded him of an obelisk (illus. p. 185, pp. 186–187). "It is a speck of black in a sundrenched landscape," he wrote in the abovementioned letter. "But it is also one of the most interesting shades of black."

Wheat Field with Reaper and Sun, 1889, oil on canvas,
28¾ x 35¾ in (73 x 92 cm), Otterlo, Kröller-Müller Museum

To Vincent, the "black" of the cypresses was in no way a negative statement about color. As in the dark colors of his night pictures, he composed the somber needles the trees wore like a coat in various color combinations, which he applied alongside each other in impasto fashion. Without a doubt, the cypress pictures from Saint-Rémy represent one of the highpoints of van Gogh's impasto painting. This is particularly true of one painting, *Starry Night* (illus. pp. 186–187), which is among his most famous works. Vincent had already heralded it to his brother during the previous year, a few weeks after his arrival in Provence. The picture shows a mighty, starry sky arching over a little town and a range of hills that, enlivened by a bizarre maelstrom of clouds, extends toward the huge, dark flame of a cypress. The nighttime landscape, evidently that of Saint-Rémy with the Alpilles hills, seems to be gripped by a mysterious force.

Through sweeps of impasto color, that energy takes form in the firmament and enlivens the image of the cypress, so that the tree, vertically crossing the pictorial action, becomes a link between heaven and earth.

Starry Night is among the most dramatic visual images that van Gogh ever created. This work has also been interpreted as a reflection of his spiritual condition, as proof of the self-destructive power of his creativity. Vincent saw the heavenly bodies as a metaphor for infinity, a realm that was not accessible to human beings until death. Thus, *Starry Night* surely illustrates how death symbolism became increasingly important to van Gogh in Saint-Rémy. In addition, the painting is vivid evidence of just how much his painting style had changed since his departure from Arles. Even if his attempts to paint from memory according to Gauguin's example may have disillusioned him, these experiences

Enclosed Field with Rising Sun (detail), 1889, oil on canvas, 28 x 35½ in (71 x 90.5 cm), private collection

▷ *Cypresses with Two Female Figures*, 1889–1890, oil on canvas, 36 x 28½ in (91.6 x 72.4 cm), Otterlo, Kröller-Müller Museum

also visibly inspired him to abstract reality more strongly in his pictures and allow more room for imagination, thereby giving expression to his feelings.

This development was accompanied by a radically altered painting style. The two-dimensional coloring based on cloisonnism, which still characterized van Gogh's work generated in Arles to a large extent, now gave way to a "graphic," expressive style whose purpose was a more dynamic method of painting in which hard contours dissipated into a lively interplay of colored lines. This new style is also characteristic of van Gogh's works painted in Saint-Rémy that did not take cypresses as their motifs, but rather pines in the hospital garden and olive trees growing nearby. Many of these works display his regular, even use of this line technique, which connects the various elements of the picture through flowing movements, and to a substantial extent visually equalizes them. The ground, people, trees, and sky collectively form a mystical, animated landscape (illus. opposite and p. 195).

NEW CRISES

During his time in Etten, Vincent had already remarked to Theo once that he regarded the trees in his pictures "as figures." And thus, even the gnarled pines and olive trees in his Saint-Rémy landscapes look like human figures, wrenchingly throwing their arms toward heaven. They are beings who, like van Gogh, despair at the suffering of their existence (illus. pp. 188, 189). For despite the promising beginning, van Gogh's "dread of life" had only temporarily lessened at the sanatorium.

Vincent suffered an unexpected and terrible attack at the end of July, apparently brought on by a short visit to Arles, in the course of which he swallowed poisonous oil paint. Whether he had suicidal intentions at this time has been disputed, but the incident resulted in van Gogh's not being allowed to leave the sanatorium for several weeks, and he was initially forbidden to enter his studio or to paint anything. Although his condition gradually stabilized, and he showed

no further symptoms of illness for weeks, a shadow lay over his stay at the clinic from that time on. Vincent's belief in a full recovery had been shaken, and his depression lastingly intensified as a result.

Van Gogh's final four self-portraits were painted in Saint-Rémy in the aftermath of the latest crisis. One of them shows him in front of a violet background with a palette in his hand, a gaunt, insecure artist with a pale, yellowish face (illus. p. 191). In another self-portrait that was done several weeks later, Vincent's countenance still shows signs of illness (illus. p. 198), but his gaze is now firm and serious. A mass of curving blue and green lines, a chaotic pattern that had apparently become part of him, surrounds his head and carries into his clothing. This picture did not bode well for the prospect of inner peace, and in the winter and springtime van Gogh actually suffered additional severe bouts of illness.

COLORS OF THE NORTH

In the stifling heat of Arles, van Gogh had sometimes used alcohol and tobacco as stimulants to rouse his senses. He hoped, in this way, to exact greater color intensity. In Saint-Rémy, the style of his pictures admittedly gained expressivity, but van Gogh also toned down the coloring and softened the contrasts. Thus, he reproduced that "well-measured temperance" that defined his daily life in the hospital. In light of his psychological condition, it was important to him to achieve greater inner peace and clarity of thought. He would henceforth "paint more gray," [599] he wrote to Theo. This plan was clearly reflected in the landscapes of those months.

In his effort to "paint more conservatively," using "pale, inconspicuous colors, broken green tones, shades of red and rusty-yellow ochre," Vincent was expressing his longing for a new beginning, the desire to "start again from the beginning with a northern palette." [601] In the monastic seclusion of Saint-Paul-de-Mausole, van Gogh looked back on the conflicting experiences he had had since leaving his homeland. And he now confronted the overall achievements of the avant-garde with the same criticism he afforded his own work. "The new gets old so quickly," he wrote to his brother from his cell. "I believe that if I were to come to Paris in my current frame of mind, I would make no distinction between a so-called dark picture and a bright impressionist picture." [593]

Starry Night, 1889,
oil on canvas, 29 x 36¼ in (73.7 x 92.1 cm)
New York, Museum of Modern Art

Olive Trees with Yellow Sky and Sun, 1889, oil on canvas,
29 x 36½ in (73.7 x 92.7 cm), Minneapolis, Minneapolis Institute of Arts,
The William Hood Dunwoody Fund

▷ *Olive Trees with the Alpilles in the Background,* 1889
oil on canvas, 28½ x 36 in (72.6 x 91.4 cm)
New York, Museum of Modern Art, Mrs. John Hay Whitney Bequest

Vincent's criticisms concerning fashionable trends in modern art became increasingly harsh. In a letter to Theo, in which he pointed out the intimate understanding of nature in the works of the "old" Barbizon masters, he stated in a provocative undertone, "Do you think that the next great Parisian who hikes out to a suburb knows as much or more about a landscape, just because he paints it in gaudier colors?" [602] Apparently Vincent's existential agitation was associated with deep artistic insecurity, as conveyed in the self-portrait with the palette. And so, in the end, he occupied himself anew with the works of his artistic forebears. As at the beginning of his artistic career, van Gogh began to work on reproductions in the fall—and in doing so, as he wrote to Theo, hoped to find solace. In his loneliness, he again sought refuge in the familiar world of pictures.

ONCE AGAIN MILLET

Between September and May, van Gogh created more than thirty paintings based on works by other artists, including several versions of the portrait of Madame Ginoux (illus. p. 190) that Gauguin had prepared as a study for his *Night Café,* which illustrates how much the collaboration with his friend was still on his mind. The focal point of the series, however, consists of twenty works in the style of Millet. He made two copies of *The Sower* straight away, and in addition to that he chose other depictions of agricultural work, along with domestic scenes by the venerated peasant painter. For example, *First Steps (after Millet)* shows a couple in a garden with an infant, a family idyll with a basis in current events. At the end of January, Theo's wife, Johanna, had given birth to a son, and he was baptized Vincent Willem, named after his uncle and godfather. But the subject also points to a hole in the artist's life, for he was not capable of having a family of his own.

Van Gogh's copying efforts were further reinforced by his state of health, which forced him to increasingly avoid painting outdoors. But the main factor could have been the self-doubt that had plagued him since his experiences in Arles. Through revisiting the great works of others, Vincent wanted to simultaneously gain new confidence and refine his work. "I want to study," he justified his plan to Theo, whom he requested to send an extensive number of etchings and woodcuts [607].

Vincent understood his efforts as much more than mere copying. He regarded his pictures as interpretations in color and compared himself to a musician who played unfamiliar compositions and placed his own personal stamp on them

in the process. "I put a black-and-white picture by Delacroix or Millet or a black-and-white reproduction of one of their works in front of me as a subject," he described his approach to Theo, "and then I improvise on it in color." [607] *Noon: Rest from Work (after Millet)* (illus. p. 192) substantiates this improvisatory freedom. While the motif—a peasant couple pausing from their work in the shade of a haystack—is a faithful reproduction of Millet's original, the strongly contrasting colors—the powerful yellow of the grain and the deep blue sky—represent an apparent reminiscence of harvest time in Arles. Such intensity of color is entirely foreign to Millet's pictures.

In van Gogh's existential uncertainty, however, he was not only receptive to Millet's spirituality, but also to Biblical themes. He thus chose reproductions of Delacroix's *Pietà* and *The Good Samaritan*, as well as Rembrandt's *The Raising of Lazarus* as models for further color improvisations (illus.

L'Arlésienne (Madame Ginoux), 1890,
oil on canvas, 25¾ x 19¼ in (65.3 x 49 cm),
Otterlo, Kröller-Müller Museum

Self-Portrait, 1889, oil on canvas,
22½ x 17 in (57 x 43.5 cm),
Washington D.C., National Gallery of Art

Noon: Rest from Work (after Millet), 1890, oil on canvas,
28¾ x 35¾ in (73 x 91 cm), Paris, Musée d'Orsay

p. 193). These paintings are the only Biblical scenes in van Gogh's entire oeuvre. What makes them especially interesting is that around the same time, van Gogh fiercely criticized Bernard and Gauguin for their images of Christ on the Mount of Olives. Vincent had once tackled this subject in Arles, but he did not complete the work.

Many art historians see his cultural background as a possible explanation for van Gogh's brusque reaction to his painter colleagues' religiously-themed compositions. In the Netherlands, which was primarily Calvinist, there was still widespread antagonism toward pictures of saints. But van Gogh criticized Bernard's and Gauguin's works not based on their subject matter, but for the things that bothered him about their approach in general, namely, their alleged or actual indifference to visible reality. "Our friend, Bernard, has probably never seen an olive tree in his life.

He avoids even the slightest suggestion of the possible and of reality, and that is not the way to synthesize." [614] Van Gogh's response consisted of a series of paintings that captured the olive harvest, which he was able to witness in Saint-Rémy in the late fall. It only appeared to be a secular theme, because Vincent's atmospheric realization certainly allowed his spiritual feeling for nature to come to light once more.

Admittedly, van Gogh's copies of works by Delacroix and Rembrandt stand in a certain contradiction to his criticisms of Bernard and Gauguin. But Vincent hardly intended these works for public consumption. He copied his role models in order to comfort himself. In the process, he seems to have lent their Biblical subjects a very private dimension. That van Gogh is again referring to himself can be inferred from the red beards with which Christ and Lazarus are portrayed,

The Raising of Lazarus (after Rembrandt), 1890, oil on canvas,
19¾ x 25½ in (50 x 65 cm), Amsterdam, Van Gogh Museum

contrary to iconographic tradition. Above all, he seems to have thematicized his own suffering, as well as the promise of mercy and salvation, in these pictures.

TAKING LEAVE OF THE SOUTH

Van Gogh's renewed connection to Millet was an expression of his increasing longing for the country of his birth. Several compositions made in the winter include people who are hoeing and digging, as well as the low peasant cottages of Brabant, which he painted from memory. In terms of style and color, however, they admittedly have little in common with his early works (illus. p. 194). Still, Vincent's pictures began to show signs of steadily distancing themselves from the south.

The magnificent picture *Blossoming Almond Tree* (illus. pp. 196–197), which van Gogh painted for his young nephew,

at first glance seems to contradict this, as it takes up a theme to which Vincent had devoted a series during his first euphoric weeks in Provence. However, it is striking that in contrast to the blooming fruit orchard from Arles, he did not place the almond branches in a particular location. The picture shows them in front of a radiant blue background with a clear spring sky in the form of a monochrome surface. The seasonal motif, which van Gogh painted from memory, does not bring up happy memories of days gone by, but is an allegory that foreshadows an unfolding life.

As a kind of greeting from the south, the painting was also partly an advance notice of his own travel plans, because van Gogh's reawakened interest in the north was certainly not limited to the aesthetic and artistic spheres, of course; after an absence of two years, he clearly felt mounting pressure to return. For months now, he had corresponded with Theo about his plans in this regard. But he did not want to return to his mother and sisters in Holland, with whom

▷ *Thatched Cottages in the Sunshine: Reminiscence of the North*, 1890,
oil on canvas on wood, 20 x 15 in (50.8 x 38.1 cm),
Merion, PA, The Barnes Foundation

he exchanged letters more frequently. Instead, he wanted to be near his brother in the environs of Paris. After both Theo and Vincent had considered and rejected several possibilities, Auvers-sur-Oise, a little village northwest of Paris, was chosen as the most suitable destination for Vincent. There, Doctor Paul Gachet, a country doctor and amateur painter, would look after him.

> *"Little by little, the surroundings here*
> *begin to oppress me more than I can tell you.*
> *Heavens, I have endured it for over a year.*
> *I must have some air;*
> *I am overwhelmed by unhappiness and*
> *boredom. Work calls, and I don't want to*
> *waste any more time here."* [631]
>
> *Vincent van Gogh to Theo, May 1890*

With a final cypress picture, van Gogh took leave of Provence (illus. opposite). The painting shows two of the dark trees united into a single, powerful solitaire in the middle of the canvas. On the edge of a cornfield, they rise up into the brightly lit night sky, splitting it in half. The treetop is framed by a pale star to one side and an orange-colored crescent moon on the other. In the foreground, two hikers are moving briskly toward the viewer, and they are followed at some distance by a carriage that has just passed a little cottage.

The symbolic aspect of this work is unmistakable. In it, Vincent brought together iconographic elements of his creativity and at the same time summed up the years that lay behind him. It is a melancholy landscape, more fantasy than reality, expressing van Gogh's longing for community and his homelessness in equal measure, his spirituality and his striving for eternity. The street becomes an allegory for a life that is not yet complete; nevertheless, a presentiment of death seems to hang over it.

On May 16, 1890, van Gogh set out on the night train, headed for yet another phase of his restless existence. This would be his last trip of any duration. Behind him lay the south of France, a place he had headed with high hopes more than two years earlier. While there, he had both reached the apex of his creativity and experienced his bitterest disappointments.

STOPOVER IN PARIS

While en route to Auvers, van Gogh stopped in Paris for a few days. There, he finally had the opportunity to meet Theo's wife, Johanna, with whom he had only exchanged letters until then, and to see his little nephew. "Jo," who as the executor of her brother-in-law's estate would later play a decisive role in van Gogh's posthumous fame, retrospectively described the positive impression Vincent made on her when they first met. He had not only been cheerful, but also appeared vital and well-groomed, with unexpectedly healthy facial color.

If this recollection is to be believed, Vincent's surprisingly good state of health may have roused thoroughly ambivalent feelings in his young sister-in-law, because her husband, who so lovingly cared for his brother, was himself not a healthy man. Debilitated by a chronic cough and still hoping to strike out on his own and be self-employed, Theo was experiencing professionally and financially uncertain times. This was not hidden from Vincent, so the family gathering was likely not quite as cheerful as Johanna described it in retrospect, at least not below the surface.

▷ *Road with Cypress and Star*, 1890,
oil on canvas, 35½ x 28⅓ in (90.6 x 72 cm),
Otterlo, Kröller-Müller Museum

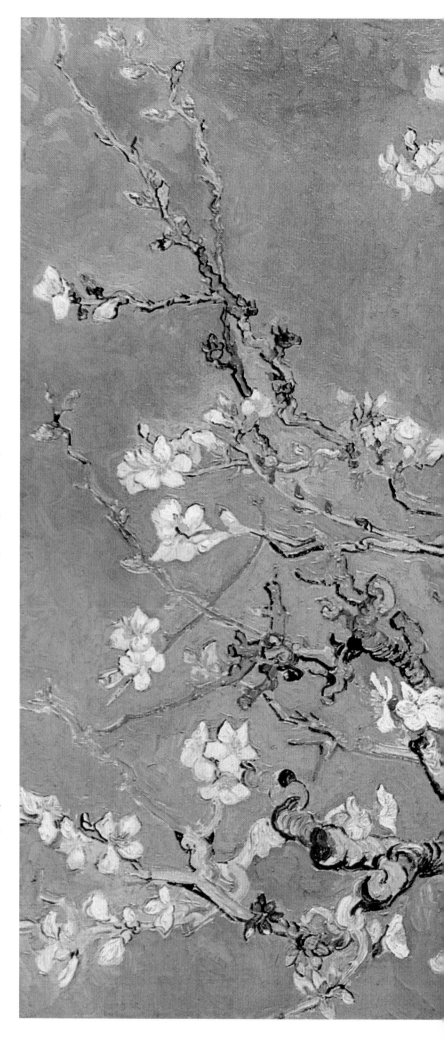

> *"Although I was sick, I still did a few small pictures from memory, which you will see later on. [They are] reminiscences of the north."* [629]
>
> *Vincent van Gogh to Theo, April 29, 1890*

Van Gogh took advantage of his visit to the French capital to meet with old acquaintances from Montmartre artist circles, and he encountered new admirers, as well. Interest in the idiosyncratic Dutchman had grown notably during his absence, in part because his pictures were increasingly visible, due mainly to his brother's efforts. In September of the previous year, Theo had presented two of Vincent's paintings—*Starry Night over the Rhone* (illus. p. 136) and *Irises* (illus. pp. 180–181)—at the Salon des Indépendants. Several weeks later, Père Tanguy exhibited a number of Vincent's works at his art supply store. In January, six of his pictures had been included in the exhibition of the avant-garde artists' group Les Vingt in Brussels. And in March 1890, when no fewer than ten van Gogh paintings were displayed at the Salon des Indépendants, Vincent was no longer an unknown, at least not in the Parisian art scene.

At the same time, the first enthusiastic reviews appeared. Dutch art critic Joseph Jacob Isaacson started things off when he feted his countryman as a "lone pioneer" in the art journal *De Portefeuille*. Albert Aurier, a critic who had close ties to the symbolists, caused a greater sensation in January when he published "Les Isolés: Vincent van Gogh," a genuine tribute to van Gogh that eloquently and insightfully described the specific qualities of his work in *Le Mercure de France*.

Vincent was not taken by surprise by the resounding interest in his work, because Theo had always kept him up to date. But as much he enjoyed the accolades and especially valued Aurier's opinions, in the end, he still doubted the legitimacy of the sudden appreciation. Personally, he still believed that he had not achieved much with his work. "I may see the possibility of a new kind of painting from afar," he wrote to Isaacson at that time, "but it was too much for me, and I will gladly return to the north." [614a] Apparently, van Gogh found all the commotion about him a bit suspect, and although he had originally intended to paint several portraits in Paris, he ended his short visit to the art mecca after just three days, and quickly departed for Auvers.

Blossoming Almond Tree, 1890,
oil on canvas, 29 x 36¼ in (73.5 x 92 cm),
Amsterdam, Van Gogh Museum

VAN GOGH AND MADNESS

The nineteenth-century cult of romantic genius made the lunatic artist into a topos, and van Gogh seems to be the perfect embodiment of that stereotype. To this day, the belief that his artistic expression and creativity mainly resulted from mental illness has lost little of its attraction. But the actual illness he suffered from has not been identified with certainty.

Self-Portrait, 1889, oil on canvas,
25½ x 21½ in (65 x 54.5 cm), Paris, Musée d'Orsay

Van Gogh's mutilation of his ear with a razor blade and his later suicide in the cornfields are surely among the most oft-repeated legends of art history. The source material that would shed light on these events is scant, to put it mildly; yet this has promoted their dissemination, rather than hindering it, making these events all the easier to incorporate into the mythmaking process. They allegedly serve as proof of the self-destructive energy that supposedly defined Vincent's inner life, and his art along with it.

It would certainly seem reasonable to view Van Gogh's acts of self-aggression in relation to the psychological disturbance that he unquestionably suffered beginning in the winter of 1888–1889, although there were signs of it even earlier. Establishing a definitive connection is more problematic, however, because van Gogh's complex clinical picture allows for numerous diagnoses. The most varied attempts have been made, some more serious than others, in an effort to explain the medical aspect of the "van Gogh mystery."

Vincent believed that his recurring episodes of ill health, or "attacks," which were accompanied by hallucinations and usually subsided after a few days, were attributable to epilepsy. He was encouraged in this assumption by his attending physicians in Arles and Saint-Rémy, Dr. Felix Rey and Dr. Théophile Peyron. It is noteworthy that research in this area of medicine was still in its infancy at the time. Nevertheless, subsequent studies have supported both doctors' assessments, so today there are still numerous advocates of the theory that van Gogh suffered from what is called temporal lobe epilepsy. Other authors, however, are of the opinion that van Gogh's illness was of a schizophrenic nature. Likewise, the widely supported diagnosis of a manic-depressive illness seems highly plausible, because it could also provide an explanation for Vincent's conspicuous mood swings and his astounding productivity.

Of course, one cannot rule out the possibility that several disease patterns overlapped, and physical conditions probably also played an important role. Van Gogh's recurring periods of neglect of his nutritional needs; his intermittently excessive consumption of alcohol, coffee, and tobacco; as well as the rather unmindful handling of poisonous pigments, solvents, and other harmful materials, at least by today's standards, may have not only caused Vincent's chronic stomach ailments, but may also have caused lasting damage to his brain.

Also conceivable is that van Gogh, who had lived with the prostitute Clasina Maria Hoornik for quite some time in The Hague and regularly frequented bordellos, at the very least while he lived in Arles, was suffering from the long-term consequences of gonorrhea or had even contracted syphilis. The latter venereal disease, which was nearly always fatal at the time, spreads to the brain in the final stage, and both syphilis and absinthe poisoning were commonplace in bohemian and artist circles in those days. Those who fell victim to syphilis included not only fellow artists Paul Gauguin and Henri de Toulouse-Lautrec, but Vincent's own brother Theo also died from Lues venerea.

Similarly, there is reason to believe that van Gogh's genetic disposition could have contributed to or even caused his suffering. After all, his younger brother, Cornelis (called Cor), also later committed suicide, and his favorite sister, Wil, spent the last forty years of her life in a psychiatric facility. Vincent had once remarked to Theo that in a particular photograph, their sister had the look of a mentally ill person.

In light of Vincent's problematic relationship with his father, it is always possible that traumatic childhood

equilibrium. It is intriguing to note that the great twentieth-century artist Salvador Dalí was also given the name of an older brother who died in infancy, and was greatly disturbed by that fact.

As sensible as many explanations may sound, there is no certain knowledge. Van Gogh's art does not display any demonstrably psychotic traits. The intense colors and distorted perspectives that are found particularly in his works from Provence have often been cited by non-academics as a direct

Kirk Douglas as Vincent: movie still from Vincente Minnelli's
Lust for Life (USA 1956)

experiences could have come into play, which would explain van Gogh's neurotic sensibility, his existential fear, and his depressive emotional state, all of which clearly come through in his letters to Theo. The older brother who died at birth, who also shared Vincent's name, played a central role in his psychoanalytic examinations, as well. The belief that he was no more than a substitute for the firstborn Vincent could have led to a disturbed sense of identity, and may have placed a lifelong burden on van Gogh's spiritual

expression of van Gogh's insanity. They can also be explained as the original creations of an extremely reflective artist, who saw the principal role of his work as that of breaking new ground in art. Vincent apparently did not believe that his psychological crises enriched his artistic creativity. "As far as I can tell, I am not actually a madman," he wrote to his brother from Arles. "You will see, in fact, that the pictures I completed in between attacks are calm and no worse than any others." [580]

FINALE: AUVERS-SUR-OISE

COMING HOME?

On May 20, 1890, Vincent arrived in Auvers-sur-Oise after a short train ride from Paris. With its vineyards, attractive country houses, and picturesque river landscapes, the little town in the Oise Valley was not only a popular weekend getaway spot for city folks in need of a rest, but also a destination for plein air painters (illus. p. 19). Charles-François Daubigny had spent his sunset years here, and many Parisian artists from impressionist circles frequented the home of Dr. Gachet, who was an avid painter and collector himself.

This doctor with an artistic streak made "a fairly eccentric impression" on van Gogh at first, as he related to Theo and Jo soon after his arrival. "But his experience as a doctor in fighting neurological maladies must keep him in balance, since it seems to me that he suffers from them at least as much as I do." [635] A widower, Dr. Gachet lived with his children, Marguerite and Paul, and he instructed van Gogh in etching techniques. In several letters, Vincent indeed called him a "friend," and even painted his portrait (illus. opposite). Nevertheless, the relationship between the two seems to have been ambivalent. "A person should not rely on Dr. Gachet in any way," Vincent stated in one of his last letters to his brother. "If one blind person is leading another, don't they both fall into the ditch?" [648] He did not pin any of his hopes for recovery on the doctor.

Gachet apparently kept his distance from his "patient" at the beginning. Instead of allowing van Gogh to move into his spacious home, he took him to a nearby guest house. Vincent left it at once, however, in search of a more economical place to sleep. And he found it, at some distance from Gachet's, on the premises of the Ravoux family inn. And so he lived the two remaining months of his life in a little garret above a village tavern.

Pages 200–201
Wheat Field Under Clouded Sky (detail), 1890, oil on canvas, 19¾ x 39½ in (50 x 100.5 cm), Amsterdam, Van Gogh Museum

▷ *Portrait of Doctor Paul Gachet*, 1890, oil on canvas, 26¾ x 22½ in (68 x 57 cm), Paris, Musée d'Orsay

His modest accommodations across from the town hall are not the only thing that may have reminded van Gogh of his childhood in Zundert. In Auvers, there were also still several old-fashioned peasant cottages with thatched roofs like the ones he was familiar with from Brabant. "It is really so very beautiful," Vincent wrote, apparently quite taken with his new surroundings. "One is really out in the country, an exceptionally picturesque area." [635] It is rather astonishing that he was apparently not disturbed at all by the mark that the proximity to Paris had clearly left on the village's appearance. "I find the modern villas and country homes of the bourgeoisie nearly as nice as the old straw cottages, which are falling to pieces." [636] Auvers offered Vincent a broad spectrum of subject matter, and it appears to have been a good fit with his creative urges. In the nine weeks that followed, van Gogh created eighty paintings, mainly landscapes and village scenes, as well as several portraits and floral still lifes.

RETURNING TO COLORS

Although van Gogh seldom indulged in illusions concerning his illness and remained skeptical that an artistic breakthrough was on the horizon that would bring with it the prospect of a substantial improvement in his financial situation, he set to work with a vengeance right after he arrived. "Something entirely new will surely happen to me in the north," [604] he conjectured to Theo while still in Saint-Rémy. During his brief stay in Paris, he had been able to take another look at his early work dating from the Holland period. Afterward, he was even more eager to discover how his perspective on the north had changed, and he was not disappointed. "I can already tell that it has done me good to have gone south," he reported to his brother after he painted his first peasant cottages (illus. pp. 206–207). "Just as I thought, I see the violet colors more intensely, wherever they are found. Auvers is positively beautiful." [636]

At the Saint-Paul-de-Mausole sanatorium, van Gogh had expressed his longing for his home by toning down the bright colors in his paintings, by painting "more gray." In

Auvers, powerful colors reappeared in his pictures. Rather than the dark Dutch color scheme that had defined his early work, he now portrayed the north in lucid colors. In the "fruitful to nearly overflowing region" [637] around Auvers, he discovered not only more intensely violet shades, but also powerful reds and radiant yellows. In the colors of his pictures, however, the luscious greens and deep blue heavens of the sultry, warm summer days are the most prominent of all. As during harvest time in Arles, Vincent exaggerated the colors so as to evoke the vitality of Provence.

At first, van Gogh found most of his motifs in the village. After the experiences of recent months, he may possibly have been afraid to work in the open fields. The peaceful views of blossoming almond trees and gardens, of handsome little houses and cottages, allow one to assume that Vincent was intent on keeping his inner demons in check. As he had written to his sister Wil in the winter, he was anxious to restrain the destructive power that "almost" made his pictures into a "cry of anguish." [W 20]

For the time being, the darkness inherent in his works from Saint-Rémy had disappeared from his paintings. His works painted in Auvers, however, seldom attained the same succinctness as those from his previous creative phases. Stylistically they exude an attractive lightness that was undoubtedly less an expression of ecstatic creativity and more a sign of sovereign command gained through years of practice. And so the works of those early summer days virtually seem to illustrate Vincent's belief that he had overcome the "illness of the south"—if only temporarily.

FINAL PORTRAITS

In Auvers, van Gogh hoped to be able to paint more portraits, but once again he found it difficult to find models. Although his daily routine resembled that of a peasant—he got up at first light to work and went to bed at sundown—Vincent apparently found no real points of contact with the local population. As in Arles, he therefore ended up painting portraits of people who, with very few exceptions, were mainly in his immediate environment. For example, he painted a half-figure portrait of his innkeepers' fifteen-year-old daughter, Adeline Ravoux, seated in front of a dark blue background (illus. p. 210). While it does not particularly bring out her individual traits, the picture portrays her rather awkward adolescent charm and shyness.

Field with Poppies, 1890,
oil on canvas, 28¾ x 36 in (73 x 91.5 cm),
The Hague, Haags Gemeentemuseum

Village Street and Steps in Auvers with Figures, 1890, oil on canvas,
20 x 28 in (51 x 71 cm), Saint Louis, Saint Louis Art Museum

Houses in Auvers, 1890, oil on canvas,
29¾ x 24⅓ in (75.6 x 61.9 cm), Boston, Museum of Fine Arts

◁ *Landscape with Carriage and Train in the Background,* 1890,
oil on canvas, 28⅓ x 35½ in (72 x 90 cm), Moscow, Pushkin Museum

The Little Arlesienne, 1890, oil on canvas,
20½ x 19½ in (51.9 x 49.5 cm), Otterlo, Kröller-Müller Museum

▷ *Young Peasant Woman with Straw Hat Sitting in the Wheat*, 1890,
oil on canvas, 36¼ x 28¾ in (92 x 73 cm), private collection

The famous *Portrait of Doctor Paul Gachet* (illus. p. 203) is another matter entirely. He and van Gogh had gotten to know each other better in the meantime, and found they had certain traits and artistic preferences in common. "His profession as a country doctor satisfies him as little as my painting does me," [637] Vincent wrote to his brother. Thus he portrayed the doctor as a kindred spirit, a melancholy man with a soulful gaze, seated at table—a man who was visibly torn between inclination and obligation, two spheres that are symbolized in the portrait by the colors red and blue.

Van Gogh also first painted Gachet's daughter, Marguerite, as a "white figure" in her father's garden (illus. p. 212). A second painting shows her seated and in profile, playing the piano. This is a delicate portrait that, interestingly enough,

does not accentuate the facial features of the twenty-one-year-old, but instead makes the white dress she wears the central pictorial element (illus. right). Molded with lavish, finely nuanced brush strokes, the article of clothing looks almost like a cloud that envelops the young woman. It is disembodied in such a way that the pianist seems to transform her surroundings into a poetic space with her music. The room seems to gain a melodic life of its own through the use of the red dots in the green background and the olive green lines in the reddish-brown floor.

The conspicuously graphic design of the composition, as well as the upright format with a height-to-width ratio of two to one, underscores the decorative aspect of this unusual portrait, which clearly differentiates itself from van Gogh's other portrait paintings. Whether Vincent had fallen in love with Marguerite has been a frequent subject of speculation. It would be anything but astonishing if he had again felt the desire for a family of his own, having his brother's in mind as a role model. Even though certain comments in his letters suggest it, a romance cannot be clearly established.

NEARING THE END

Some of the reasons why van Gogh did not ultimately find peace in Auvers are verifiable. For one thing, his letters clearly state how disturbed Vincent was by his brother's plans to start a business of his own. He saw his own financial situation as threatened by the risky undertaking, and at the same time, he became even more keenly aware of how he had limited Theo's options from the very beginning by relying on him so heavily for economic support. He found it almost intolerable that because of him, Theo's own family—his wife and child—would have to tighten their belts. And Theo's frightful state of health undoubtedly further increased Vincent's uncertainty.

At the same time, van Gogh was apparently disappointed that his return to the north had not brought about the closeness with Theo that he longed for, because his brother was too preoccupied with business and family matters. When Theo's young son also became seriously ill, Vincent urgently pressed his brother to move out to the country, near him, so that the child could grow up in a healthy environment. This was apparently not an entirely unselfish proposition, and was certainly not one that Theo could dismiss offhand. Vincent's emotional cocktail of guilt, loneliness, anxiety about the future, and fear of renewed attacks seems to have become explosive within a matter of weeks. Theo, who knew Vincent all too well, feared an impending crisis in mid-July, and his fears were confirmed shortly thereafter in a terrible way.

It was characteristic of van Gogh to let the existential insecurity that increasingly gripped him flow into his work. In the painting *The Church at Auvers* (illus. p. 213), for example,

Marguerite Gachet at the Piano, 1890, oil on canvas, 40⅓ x 19¾ in (102.5 x 50 cm), Basel, Kunstmuseum Basel

"I have discovered that this canvas goes very well next to another horizontal one of wheat [*Wheat Fields near Auvers*], as one is vertical and in tones of pink, while the other is pale green and greenish-yellow, complementary colors to the pink. But we're still far from the point when people will understand the curious relationship between one element of nature and another, which still explain and enhance one another." [645] Vincent van Gogh to Theo, June 1890

◁ *Portrait of Adeline Ravoux*, 1890, oil on canvas, 29 x 21½ in (73.7 x 54.6 cm), private collection

Marguerite Gachet in the Garden, 1890, oil on canvas,
18 x 21¾ in (46 x 55.5 cm), Paris, Musée d'Orsay

▷ *The Church at Auvers*, ca. 1890, oil on canvas,
37 x 29⅓ in (94 x 74.5 cm), Paris, Musée d'Orsay

his agitation and disorientation appear to be reproduced in the distorted contours of the astonishingly massive sacred structure and in the parting-of-the-ways motif. Both the motif and the perspective are reminiscent of the old church tower in Nuenen that had first led Vincent to reflect on his father's death, the dwindling power of the church, and the spirituality of simple country folk, as also expressed in Millet's pictures. In his late works, van Gogh returned to earlier motifs and themes or copied his role models, lending the paintings addi tional complexity. His work thus remained ambiguous and suspenseful until the end of his creative activity, as his personal situation once again intensified.

These elements are also evident in a last series of landscapes, which an Gogh began in June, for which he chose a wide horizontal format. Six years earlier, in Nuenen, he had utilized a similar format for his Millet-inspired paintings of peasants working in the fields, which themselves were based on designs he had generated for a series of wall paintings. The works from Auvers, however, were largely inspired by Daubigny's landscapes. Van Gogh had visited his nearby estate and recorded it in two landscape-format paintings (illus. p. 214). But the actual series consisted of wide panoramas that showed fields spreading over the lowlands above the Oise River Valley (illus p. 215 ff.).

In a letter from mid-July that Vincent drafted on the day after his return from a short, turbulent visit to Theo and Jo in Paris, he described the aim he was pursuing as "cornfields stretching endlessly under a troubled sky . . . I have not shied

away from trying to express sadness and the greatest possible loneliness," he explained to his brother. Shortly thereafter he added, "These canvases will tell you what I cannot say in words, namely, how healthy and invigorating I find country life." [649] The pictures convey Vincent's lifelong love of nature as well as his existential loneliness (illus. p. 215 top, pp. 216–217). The emptiness of these panoramas is unmistakable. There is not a single person to be found in them, not even one of the peasants that so often served as identification figures in van Gogh's works. The spiritual peace and harmony that Millet professed to have found in his peasant-painter existence eluded van Gogh throughout his entire life.

DEATH

Wheat Field with Crows (illus. pp. 218–219) belongs to this last series of landscape panoramas. Its fame is due in large part to the supposition, still widely held, that it was the picture van Gogh painted immediately prior to his suicide. This erroneous belief can be attributed to the melodramatic portrayal of events in Vincente Minnelli's famous film about van Gogh, *Lust for Life*. According to the script, Vincent was painting when he fell prey to the insanity that caused him to fatally shoot himself with a revolver. This legend has undoubtedly endured due to the hauntingly sinister symbolism of the painting,

▷ *Wheat Field Under Clouded Sky*, 1890, oil on canvas,
19¾ x 39½ in (50 x 100.5 cm), Amsterdam, Van Gogh Museum

▷ *Cows (After Jordaens)*, 1890, oil on canvas,
21⅓ x 26 in (55 x 65 cm), Lille, Musée des Beaux-Arts

in which the dark, stormy sky above the field, the soaring birds, and the three diverging paths seem to bespeak van Gogh's longing for death. Nevertheless, questions about his last work remain unresolved, as do many other questions that touch on his death.

What is certain is that on July 27, 1890, van Gogh returned home late in the evening from a visit to the tavern belonging to the Ravouxs. He retired to his room, clearly in considerable pain, whereupon the innkeepers notified Mazery, the town doctor, and Dr. Gachet. Vincent told the doctors that he had shot himself in the chest. Since neither Gachet nor Mazery felt capable of removing the bullet, all they could do was bandage the wound. The next morning, Gachet notified Theo, who immediately rushed to Auvers and remained by his wounded brother's bedside until Vincent died in the early morning hours of July 29. According to Theo's statement, his brother's last words were, *"la tristesse durera toujours"* (the sadness will last forever).

Vincent's dead face was captured in a small drawing by Gachet (illus. foldout). The burial took place the very next day,

Daubigny's Garden, 1890, oil on canvas,
22 x 40 in (56 x 101.5 cm), Basel, Staechelin Familienstiftung

Landscape at Auvers in the Rain, 1890, oil on canvas,
19¾ x 39⅓ in (50 x 100 cm), Cardiff, National Museum of Wales

at three in the afternoon, in the village cemetery at the edge of the fields. Present was a small group of mourners, among them Bernard, Laval, "Père" Tanguy, and Lucien Pissarro, who had arrived on short notice from Paris.

There are very few reports concerning van Gogh's final hours, and those that do exist hardly shed light on the circumstances of his suicide. According to Gachet's and Theo's descriptions, Vincent faced death calmly. To both of them, it was beyond question that he wanted to die, although it also seems entirely plausible that Vincent's act was intended only as a "cry for help." In his loneliness, he may have inflicted the wound on himself in order to get his brother's attention. However, the idea of an intentional suicide made van Gogh into a martyr, and it was as a martyr that he would make a name for himself posthumously.

POSTHUMOUS RENOWN

After Vincent's death, just as soon as he returned to Paris, Theo began to safeguard his brother's life's work from obscurity. With Bernard's help, Theo organized a provisional retrospective of Vincent's work in his own apartment, the first exhibition that was devoted exclusively to van Gogh. Theo also contacted art critic Albert Aurier, who had written such a positive review of Vincent's artwork, in hopes of convincing him to write his brother's biography. But Theo's activities came to an abrupt end in September, when the state of his health suddenly worsened. In addition to a chronic cough, he also began to suffer from hallucinations. Finally, after he had attacked his wife and child, he was committed to a Paris hospital for the mentally ill and one month later was taken to a clinic in Utrecht. He died there on January 25, 1891. According to medical records, the cause of Theo van Gogh's death was syphilis.

Upon Theo's death, the majority of Vincent van Gogh's oeuvre became the property of Theo's wife, Johanna. Although the multitude of letters of condolence Theo had received after Vincent's burial testify to the widespread interest that his artwork had already attracted among those involved in the art scene, the estate was undoubtedly of little commercial value at that time.

Johanna moved to Holland with her son and her cumbersome inheritance. From there, through great perseverance and exceptional skill, she succeeded in making Vincent's art famous by means of exhibitions and intensive public relations. She first established his reputation in Holland and France, and then in Germany as well. Barely fifteen years after his death, his works had not only become highly sought-after

collectors' items that fetched incredibly high prices in the art market, but they also became an important source of inspiration for new avant-garde art, fauvism, and expressionism. At the same time, a wider public began to take interest in Vincent van Gogh.

The extensive correspondence that had gone back and forth between Vincent and Theo played a significant role in this, as did Bernard's early publication of several excerpts from their letters in *Le Mercury de France* in 1893. Johanna sorted and dated the extensive correspondence. She approved only a small portion of it for publication at first, before finally issuing the three-volume *Letters of Vincent Van Gogh* in 1914. She took her own interests and those of the family into account by withholding certain passages in the correspondance and sometimes even entire letters. Because Theo's widow also provided the volumes of letters with comprehensive introductions, she undoubtedly

played a significant role in the romanticization of Vincent and Theo that increasingly determined public perception of them. Her marketing efforts further fed the public's mindset when, on the occasion of the publication of the letters, she allowed her husband's remains to be moved to the Auvers Cemetery, where they have since rested next to Vincent's.

When Johanna died in 1925 and her son, Vincent Willem, took over his uncle's bequest, Vincent van Gogh was already the most famous of all modern artists. His paintings were valuable assets to the most important collections worldwide, and their high market value resulted in more and more forgeries. Biographies and memoirs by contemporaries and family members achieved wide circulation, and consolidated the idea of a genius who had seemingly appeared from nowhere. Parallel to the progressive creation of this legend, the emerging field of art history began to tap into van Gogh's life and work.

Today, Vincent van Gogh is both an icon of global popular culture and one of the most intensively researched artists of all time. His works sell at auction for amounts in the tens of millions. Nevertheless, a majority of his works are accessible to everyone, and something new can always be discovered in them, whether in the form of books and prints or firsthand in the great museums and public collections of the world. Van Gogh's pictures belong to all humanity today, thereby fulfilling one of the central concerns of his wonderful art.

Pages 218–219
Wheat Field with Crows, 1890,
oil on canvas, 20 x 40½ in (50.5 x 103 cm),
Amsterdam, Van Gogh Museum

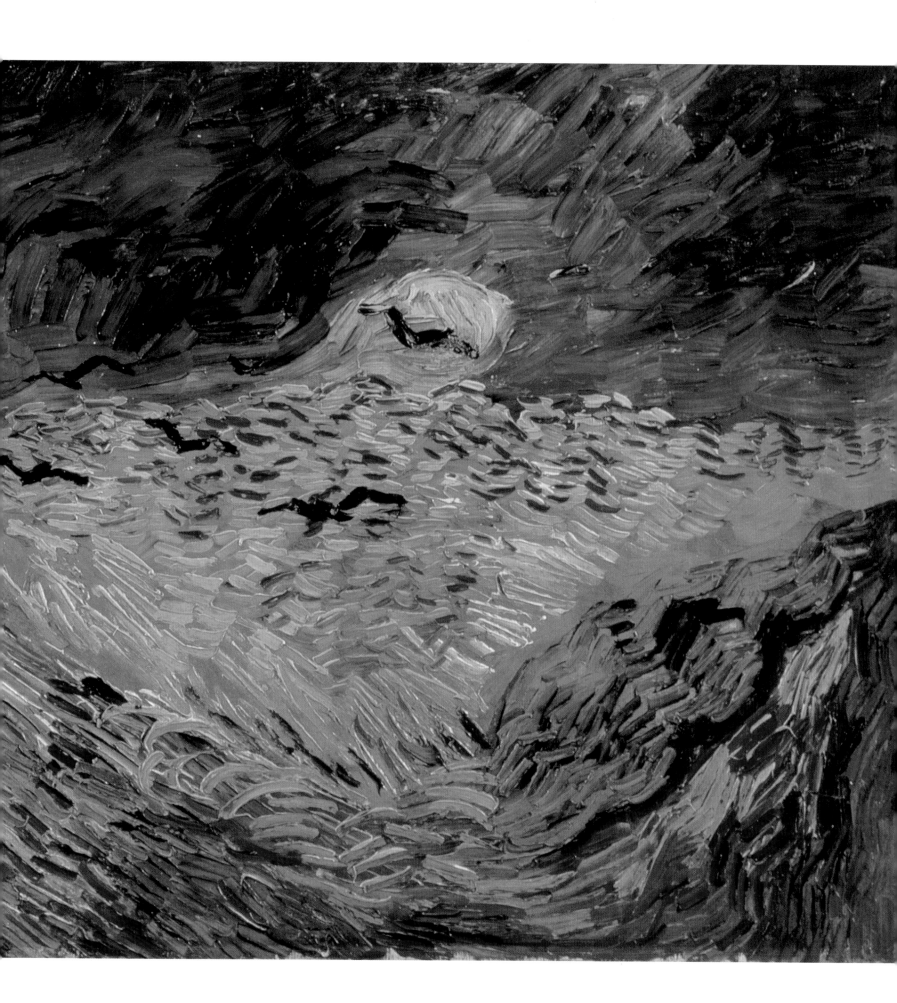

INDEX OF ILLUSTRATED WORKS
BY VINCENT VAN GOGH

(the abbreviation FT stands for foldout timeline)

SELECTED LITERATURE

Compendiums of van Gogh's works

Faille, Jacob-Baart de la. *The Works of Vincent Van Gogh: His Paintings and Drawings.* Amsterdam and New York, 1970.

Hulsker, Jan: *The New Complete van Gogh: Paintings, Drawings, Sketches.* Thoroughly updated and expanded edition of the *Catalogue Raisonné,* 1st ed. 1977. Philadelphia, 1996.

Van Gogh's letters

Gogh Vincent van. *Sämtliche Briefe.* New translation by Eva Schumann, ed. Fritz Erpel, six volumes. (East) Berlin, 1965 (vol. 1–4), 1968 (vol. 5–6).

Biographies, monographs, and exhibition catalogues

Arnold, Matthias. *Vincent van Gogh. Biographie.* Munich, 1993.

——. *Vincent van Gogh. Werk und Wirkung.* Munich, 1995.

——. *Van Gogh und seine Vorbilder. Eine künstlerische Selbstfindung.* Munich and New York, 1997.

Brettell, Richard R. *Impression: Painting Quickly in France, 1869–1890.* New Haven and London, 1990.

Burmeister, Andreas, Christoph Heilmann and Michael F. Zimmermann. *Barbizon. Malerei der Natur – Natur der Malerei.* Munich, 1999.

Dippel, Andrea. *Impressionismus.* Cologne, 2002.

Druick, Douglas W. and Peter Kort Zegers in collaboration with Britt Salvesen. *Van Gogh and Gauguin: The Studio of the South* (catalog for an exhibition at the Art Institute of Chicago and the Van Gogh Museum, Amsterdam). Chicago, 2001.

Forrester, Viviane. *Van Gogh ou l'enterrement dans les blés.* Paris, 1984. (German edition: *Van Gogh oder das Begräbnis im Weizen,* trans. from French by Gerd Stange. Hamburg, 2003.)

Gauguin, Paul. *Avant et aprés.* Paris, 1925.

Heugten, Sjraar van. *Van Gogh. Die Zeichnungen* (catalog for an exhibition at the Van Gogh Museum, Amsterdam, and the Metropolitan Musuem of Art, New York). Amsterdam/Stuttgart, 2005.

Koldehoff, Stefan. *Van Gogh. Mythos und Wirklichkeit. Die Wahrheit über den teuersten Maler der Welt.* Cologne, 2003.

Költzsch, Georg-W., ed. *Vincent van Gogh und die Moderne 1890–1914* (catalog for an exhibition at the Folkwang Museum, Essen, Germany, and at the Rijksmuseum Vincent van Gogh, Amsterdam). Freren, Germany, 1990.

Lobstein, Dominique. *Les salons au XIXe siècle: Paris, capitale des arts.* Paris, 2006.

Meedendorp, Teit. *Drawings and Graphics of Vincent van Gogh in the Kröller-Müller Museum* (exhibition catalog). Amsterdam, 2007.

Meier-Graefe, Julius. *Vincent van Gogh. Der Roman eines Gottsuchers.* Munich, 1910.

Nigg, Walter. *Vincent van Gogh. Der Blick in die Sonne. Ein biographischer Essay.* Zurich, 2003.

Pickvance, Ronald. *Van Gogh in Arles* (catalog for an exhibition at the Metropolitan Museum of Art). New York, 1984.

Rewald, John. *Post-Impressionism, From Van Gogh to Gauguin.* New York, 1956.

Saint Louis Art Museum, Städelsches Kunstinstitut and Städtische Galerie, Frankfurt, ed. *Vincent van Gogh and the Painters of the Petit Boulevard* (catalog for an exhibition at the Saint Louis Art Museum and the Städelsches Kunstinstitut, Frankfurt, Germany). New York, 2001.

Schneider, Angela, Anke Daemgen, and Gary Interow, eds. *Französische Meisterwerke des 19. Jahrhunderts aus dem Metropolitan Museum of Art, New York* (catalog for an exhibition at the Neue Nationalgalerie, Berlin). Berlin, 2007.

Stolwijk, Chris, Sjraar van Heugten, Leo Jansen and Andreas Blühm, ed.s, assisted by Nienke Bakker. *Mit den Augen von Vincent van Gogh. Seine Wahlverwandtschaften und sein Kunstempfinden* (catalog for the exhibition "Vincents Wahlverwandtschaften: Van Goghs Musée Imaginaire" at the Van Gogh Museum, Amsterdam). Amsterdam/Stuttgart, 2003.

Sund, Judy. *True to Temperament: Van Gogh and French Naturalist Literature.* Cambridge, 1992.

Walther, Ingo F. and Rainer Metzger. *Vincent van Gogh. Sämtliche Werke.* 2 volumes. Cologne, 1989.

Welsh-Ovcharov, Bogomila. *Vincent van Gogh and the Birth of Cloisonism* (catalog for an exhibition at the Art Gallery of Ontario, Toronto, and at the Rijksmuseum Vincent van Gogh, Amsterdam). Toronto, 1981.

Wolf, Norbert. *Epochen der Kunst. 19. Jahrhundert.* Stuttgart, 2002.

All of the quotations in the text are taken from the collected letters of Vincent van Gogh (see above for bibliographic information). The number of each letter is given in square brackets in each case. Additional support for the English translations was drawn from the following source:

Douma, Michael, curator. "Van Gogh's Letters, Unabridged and Annotated." Ed. Robert Harrison. *WebExhibits.* Institute for Dynamic Educational Advancement, Washington, DC. October 1, 2008. <http://www.webexhibits.org/vangogh/>.

PICTURE CREDITS

© 2004. Photo Art Resource / Scala, Florenz: 52/53

© 2006. Photo Art Resource / Scala, Florenz: Cover, 196/197

© akg images, Berlin: 8, 11 l., 11 c., 11 r., 36 (Erich Lessing), 38, 42/43, 46/47, 54 t., 57, 58, 59, 61, 66/67, 69, 74, 78, 80 (Erich Lessing), 81 (Erich Lessing), 91 (Laurent Lecat), 94/95, 97, 98, 107 (Erich Lessing), 111 (Erich Lessing), 114, 116, 119, 120, 120/121, 123 (Erich Lessing), 127, 128/129 (Erich Lessing), 131, 142, 148/149, 174, 178, 182, 193, 206 t., Foldout: 31. t., 31. b., 3 r. t., 3 r. b., 4 r. t., 5 l., 5 c.

© akg-images / CDA / Guillemot: 26/27

© akg-images / Electa: 44, 189, 190

© Art Institute of Chicago, Chicago / Giraudon / Bridgeman Berlin: 72/73

© Artothek, Weilheim: 68, 78/79 (Hans Hinz), 88, 132, 157, 160/161, 164, 165, 180/181, 208 (Hans Hinz), 214 (Hans Hinz), 218/219, Foldout: 2/7

© The Barnes Foundation, Merion, PA / Bridgeman Berlin: 194

© Bettmann / Corbis, Düsseldorf: 188, 199, Foldout: 5 r., 6 r.

© Blauel / Artothek, Weilheim: 45, 171

© Blauel / Gnamm / Artothek, Weilheim: 82, 115, 155, 183, 195

© Bridgeman Berlin: 2, 4, 6/7, 9, 10, 12, 15, 17, 19, 30, 32 r., 42, 48, 51, 54 b., 63, 75, 76 l., 76 r., 84/85, 86, 87 b., 89, 90, 102, 108/109, 124, 126, 133, 136, 138, 139, 140/141, 143, 145, 146, 152, 153, 158, 168, 169, 172/173, 175, 176/177, 185, 186/187, 192, 200/201, 203, 209, 211, 212, 215 t. 215 b., Foldout: 1, 3 M t., 3 c. b., 4 l. t., 6 l. b., 6 c., 8

© Brooklyn Museum of Art / Gift of Anna Ferris, New York / Bridgeman Berlin: 96

© Christie's / Artothek, Weilheim: 117, 122, 150, 154, 210

© Christie's Images / Bridgeman Berlin: 156

© Christie's Images / Corbis, Düsseldorf: Foldout: 4 l. b.

© The Detroit Institute of Arts / City of Detroit Purchase / Bridgeman Berlin: 103

© Dulwich Picture Gallery, London / Bridgeman Berlin: 16

© Fitzwilliam Museum, University of Cambridge, UK / Bridgeman Berlin: 60

© Flammarion / Bridgeman Berlin: 125

© Fogg Art Museum, Harvard University Art Museums / Bequest from the Collection of Maurice Wertheim, Class 1906, Cambridge, MA / Bridgeman Berlin; 22/23, 144

© Getty Images, Munich: Foldout: 4 r. b.

© Haags Gemeentemuseum, The Hague / Bridgeman Berlin: 13, 33 r., 204/205

© Imagno / Artothek, Weilheim: 195, Foldout: 4 c.

© Lefevre Fine Art Ltd., London / Bridgeman Berlin: 50, 71, 130, 135, Foldout: 6 l. t.

© Joseph S. Martin / Artothek, Weilheim: 70, 159

© Francis G. Mayer / Corbis, Düsseldorf: 184, 191

© M.G.M / Album / akg images, Berlin: 64

© Museum of Fine Arts / Bequest of John T. Spaulding, Boston, MA / Bridgeman Berlin: 207

© Museum of Fine Arts / Gift of Quincy Adams Shaw, through Quincy Adams Shaw, Jr. and Mrs Marian Shaw Haughton, Boston, MA / Bridgeman Berlin: 14

© Museum of Fine Arts / Gift of Robert Treat Paine II, Boston, MA / Bridgeman Berlin: 134

© National Museum and Gallery of Wales, Cardiff / Bridgeman Berlin: 216/217

© Micheline Pelletier / Sygma / Corbis, Düsseldorf: 65

© 2004. photo of Philadelphia Museum of Art / Art Resource / Scala, Florenz: 163

© Reuters / Corbis, Düsseldorf: 106

© Roger-Viollet, Paris / Bridgeman Berlin: 179

© 1990. Photo Scala, Florence: 206 b.

© 2005. Photo Scala, Florence / HIP: 166

© 2006. Photo Scala, Florence (Félicien Faillet) / Bildarchiv Preußischer Kulturbesitz, Berlin : 92/93

© Sotheby's / akg-images, Berlin: 21

© Stichting Kröller-Müller Museum, Otterlo: 18, 24, 32 l., 34/35, 55, 77

© Stichting Van Gogh Museum, Amsterdam: 25, 28/29, 31, 37, 39, 40/41, 49, 56, 62, 83, 87 t., 99, 104, 112/113

© Ken Welsh / Bridgeman Berlin: 118

© G. Westermann / Artothek, Weilheim: 162

Bruce M. White © Trustees of Princeton University: 151

© Whitford & Hughes, London / Bridgeman Berlin: 20

© Peter Willi / Artothek, Weilheim: 100, 101, 136, 147, 198, 213

PUBLISHING INFORMATION

This is a Parragon Publishing book

Copyright © Parragon Books Ltd 2008
Parragon
Queen Street House
4 Queen Street
Bath BA 1 1HE, UK

Conception and Editorial Team: Michael Konze, Lioba Waleczek, Cologne
Design: Elisabeth Hardenbicker, Cologne
Reproduction: farbo prepress, Cologne

Copyright © 2008 for the English edition
English edition produced by APE Int'l., Richmond, VA
Translation from German: Linda Marianiello
Editing of English edition: Tammi Reichel

ISBN 978-1-4075-4273-7
Printed in China

Illus. page 2: *Self-Portrait with Bandaged Ear and Pipe*, 1889, oil on canvas, 20 x 17¾ in (51 x 45 cm), private collection

Illus. page 4: *Still Life: Vase with Fifteen Sunflowers* (detail), 1888, oil on canvas, 36¼ x 28¾ in (92.1 x 73 cm), London, National Gallery

Foldout:
Illus. page 1: *Self-Portrait*, 1887, oil on paper, 13 x 9 in (32 x 23 cm), Otterlo, Kröller-Müller Museum

Illus. pages 2/7: *Irises* (detail), 1889, oil on canvas, 28 x 36½ in (71 x 93 cm), Los Angeles, J. Paul Getty Museum

Illus. page 8: *Two Lovers* (fragment), 1888, oil on canvas, 12¾ x 9 in (32.5 x 23 cm), private collection

VAN GOGH AND HIS TIMES

Biography

Philips de Koninck *Dutch Landscape*, 1655, oil on canvas, 52¾ x 65¼ in (134 x 165.8 cm), Bucharest, National Art Museum

1877 Vincent's parents convince him to take a position as a bookseller's assistant in Dordrecht. He remains there for three months, then goes to Amsterdam in May to prepare for theological studies.

1878 Van Gogh breaks off his studies and attends an evangelical school in Brussels for three months. When he is deemed unqualified, he travels on his own to the Belgian coal mining area of Borinage, where he serves as a lay preacher to the needy community of miners.

1879 In January, the evangelical school authorizes van Gogh to work as a lay preacher for six months. When his contract is not renewed, he continues the work anyway, under enormous hardship. He begins drawing in earnest.

1880 Vincent walks more than forty miles to Courrières, France, to visit the painter Jules Breton. This trip strengthens his resolve to become an artist. Theo, who was working at Goupil in Paris, will support him financially from this point on. In the fall, Vincent enrolls in courses at the Academy of Art in Brussels. He becomes friends with the painter Anthon G.A. Ridder van Rappard.

1881 In the spring, van Gogh returns to his parents' home, which is now in Etten. Inspired by Millet, he draws pastoral motifs and landscapes. He falls in love with his widowed cousin Kee, who rejects his offer of marriage. His relationship with his father worsens, and Vincent breaks with the church.

1882 Vincent moves to The Hague to study oil painting with his cousin, Anton Mauve. He shares his home with the prostitute Clasina Maria Hoornik (also known as Sien), and produces many drawings and water-

Vincent van Gogh *Prayer Before the Meal*, 1882, pencil, chalk, ink, and watercolor on paper, 23½ x 19¾ in (60 x 50 cm), private collection

colors of peasants. His Uncle Cor, also an art dealer, commissions a series of cityscapes from him.

Culture

1864 Henri de Toulouse-Lautrec is born in Albi, in the south of France, on November 24.

1867 Paul Durand-Ruel founds his art dealership in the Rue Lafitte. The brothers Charles and Edmond de Goncourt publish their novel *Manette Salomon*.

1868 Émile Bernard comes into the world on April 24 in Lille, France.

1869 Alphonse Daudet's *Letters from My Mill* is published, as is Flaubert's *The Sentimental Education*.

1872 In Le Havre, Claude Monet paints *Impression, Sunrise*, the painting that gives impressionism its name. Eadweard Muybridge founds motion study photography.

1874 The first Impressionist Exhibition takes place on the Boulevard des Capucines in Paris. Émile Zola publishes *The Belly of Paris*.

1875 Jean-François Millet dies on January 20 in Barbizon; shortly thereafter, Jean-Baptiste Corot dies on February 22 in Paris. Also in Paris, the building of the Basilica of Sacre-Coeur begins and

Pierre-Auguste Renoir *Portrait of Claude Monet*, 1875, oil on canvas, 33½ x 23¾ in (85 x 60.5 cm), Paris, Musée d'Orsay

Georges Bizet's opera *Carmen* premieres. The Paris Opéra (Opéra Garnier) opens its doors.

1877 Zola publishes *L'Assommoir* (The Bludgeon). The third Impressionist Exhibition is held, this time in a residence in the Rue le Peletier. Leo Tolstoy publishes his novel *Anna Karenina*. Courbet dies in exile in La-Tour-de-Peiltz, Switzerland, on December 31.

1878 Charles Daubigny dies on February 19 in Paris. Seurat begins his studies at the École des Beaux-Arts. Friedrich Nietzsche publishes *Human, All Too Human*.

1879 The fourth Impressionist Exhibition is held in the Avenue de l'Opéra. Zola's *Nana* appears as a serial novel in the journal *Le Voltaire*. Honoré Daumier dies on February 10 in Valmondois. The first exhibition of the *Société d'aquarellistes français* (Society of French Watercolorists) is held.

1880 The fifth Impressionist Exhibition takes place in the Rue des Pyramides. The state turns

History

over central Europe. Werner von Siemens builds the first dynamo machine.

1867 Austria and Hungary become a double monarchy. Paris hosts a second World's Fair. Russian Czar Alexander II sells Alaska to the USA for US $7.2 million.

Karl Marx, 1867

Karl Marx publishes *Das Kapital* (*Capital*).

1869 Opening of the Suez Canal.

1870 The German-French War breaks out. Napoleon III abdicates, and the Third Republic is proclaimed.

1871 France capitulates. Wilhelm I is proclaimed German emperor at Versailles. The Parisian Communard uprising begins in March, only to be brutally supressed two months later.

1873 The World's Fair is held in Vienna. The economic boom of the *Gründerzeit* (founding period) ends in a worldwide depression. The Netherlands declares war on the sultan of Aceh in Sumatra. The Three Emperors' League between Germany, Austria-Hungary, and Russia is created in Vienna, thus averting the rapprochement between France and Russia that Bismarck feared.

1875 The French National Assembly adopts the Constitution of the Third Republic, which has existed since 1871. The British acquire the majority of shares in the Suez Canal.

General Custer's Last Stand on June 25, 1876, lithograph, ca. 1882

1876 The World's Fair is held in Philadelphia. Alexander Graham Bell patents the telephone. A rare Native American victory over the US Army takes place June 25–26th at the Battle of the Little Big Horn in Montana: the Sioux and Cheyenne, led by Sitting Bull and Crazy Horse, wipe out General George A. Custer's regiment.

Biography	Culture	History

Biography

1853 — Vincent Willem van Gogh is born on March 30 in Groot-Zundert, North Brabant. He is the oldest of the six surviving children born to protestant pastor Theodorus van Gogh and his wife, Anna Cornelia.

1857 — Vincent's brother Theo is born on May 1.

1861 — Van Gogh attends the village school in Zundert.

1864 — Just after he turns eleven, Vincent leaves home to attend the boarding school in Zevenbergen, where he learns several foreign languages.

1866 — Vincent, now thirteen, transfers to the Willem II State Boarding School in Tilburg, where he receives drawing lessons.

Vincent at the age of 13

1868 — Van Gogh ends his schooling at the age of fifteen and returns to Zundert for seventeen months.

1869 — Vincent begins an apprenticeship in The Hague at a branch of Goupil & Cie, an art dealership of which his Uncle Cent was a co-owner, and van Gogh's enthusiasm for art and literature is awakened. He is especially interested in the Old Dutch Masters, but also in the plein air painters of the Barbizon and Hague schools.

1872 — Vincent and Theo begin their correspondence.

1873 — Theo begins an apprenticeship as an art dealer in the Brussels branch of Goupil & Cie. Vincent moves to London, visiting Paris beforehand.

1874 — Van Gogh is involved in an unhappy love affair. He immerses himself in Bible study, neglecting his work. He is moved to the Goupil head office in Paris in the fall and, in May 1875, that becomes permanent.

Vincent's Uncle Cent, ca. 1880

1876 — Vincent's religiosity takes an extreme turn. He resigns his position in April and goes to England to work as an assistant schoolmaster and preacher.

Culture

1848 Paul Gauguin is born in Paris, France, on June 7.

Gustave Courbet, *Funeral at Ornans*, 1849–1850, oil on canvas, 124 x 263 in (315 x 668 cm), Paris, Musée d'Orsay

1849 Jean-François Millet moves into the Barbizon artists' colony. Gustave Courbet paints the seminal work of the realism movement, *Funeral at Ornans*. Katsushika Hokusai dies on May 10 in Edo, Japan.

1850 Millet paints *The Sower*.

1851 The first World's Fair is held in London.

1853 The last volume of Jules Michelet's seven-volume *History of the French Revolution* appears.

1855 The World Exhibition is held in Paris. Courbet's efforts to establish an independent salon attract little interest.

1857 Charles Baudelaire's collection of poetry *Fleurs du mal* (Flowers of Evil) and Gustave Flaubert's novel *Madame Bovary* are published.

1858 Georges-Pierre Seurat is born in Paris on December 2.

1860 The last of the five volumes of John Ruskin's work *The Modern Painters* appears.

1861 Louis Anquetin is born in Étrépagny, France, on January 2.

1862 The World's Fair is held in London. Victor Hugo publishes his novel *Les Misérables*.

1863 Edvard Munch is born on January 23 in Løten, Norway. Édouard Manet paints *The Breakfast in the Green* and *Olympia*. *Le Figaro* prints Charles Baudelaire's *The Painter of Modern Life*, a famous essay about illustrator Constantin Guys. In Paris, Eugène Delacroix dies on August 18 and Paul Signac is born on November 11.

Édouard Manet *Olympia*, 1863, oil on canvas, 51⅓ x 74¾ in (130.5 x 190 cm), Paris, Musée d'Orsay

History

1848 The February Revolution in Paris leads to democratic uprisings in all of Europe. Karl Marx and Friedrich Engels publish *The Communist Manifesto*. A constitutional amendment in the Netherlands prepares the way for a parliamentarian monarchy.

1853 The Crimean War, the first instance of modern trench warfare, breaks out between Russia and the Ottoman Empire. France, Great Britain, and the Kingdom of Sardinia support the Ottomans.

1854 The USA forces a trade agreement on Japan, thereby opening the empire to the West.

Philippe Benoist and Eugène Guérard, *Paris, International Exposition of 1855: The Palais d'Industrie and Champs Elysées*, wood engraving based on a contemporary lithograph

1856 The Crimean War ends with the Treaty of Paris, in which Russia recognizes Turkey's independence and territorial integrity.

1859 The defeat of the Austrians at the Battle of Solferino ends the Sardinian War and smooths the way for the unification of Italy.

1861 The United States Civil War breaks out.

1861 Wilhelm I becomes king of Prussia.

1863 The Communist International and the International Red Cross are founded.

1864 The German-Danish War breaks out, and Austria sides with Prussia.

1865 The northern states emerge victorious in the American Civil War. President Abraham Lincoln is assassinated. Gregor Mendel formulates his Laws of Genetics. German chemist Friedrich August Kekulé von Stradonitz publicizes his theory on the structure of benzene.

1866 The Austro-Prussian War ends with the defeat of the Hapsburgs. Prussia gains ascendancy

The assassination of Abraham Lincoln by John Wilkes Booth on April 14, 1865, contemporary wood engraving